Life Support

JULIA COPUS was born in London and now lives in Somerset. Author of four collections of poetry, she has won many awards for her work, including First Prize in the National Poetry Competition and the Forward Prize for Best Single Poem (2010). In 2018 she was made a Fellow of the Royal Society of Literature.

Life Support

100 poems to reach for
on dark nights

Edited by
Julia Copus

An Anima Book

9 7 5 3 1 2 4 6 8

A catalogue record for this book is available from
the British Library.

ISBN (PB): 9781788542845
ISBN (E): 9781788542821

Typeset by Adrian McLaughlin

Printed and bound by CPI Group (UK) Ltd,
Croydon, CRO 4YY

Head of Zeus Ltd
First Floor East
5–8 Hardwick Street
London EC1R 4RG

WWW.HEADOFZEUS.COM

ex tenebris lux

Contents

Another Self

And for That Minute a Blackbird Sang

Visible, Invisible

Introduction

'We read to know we are not alone.' So screenwriter William Nicholson had C. S. Lewis say in his 1993 film *Shadowlands*. Certain poems can provide a particularly powerful type of company – whether because of their concision, the incantatory magic of their soundscapes, or the visual power of their imagery and associations. You will find many such poems in the pages of this book. Its subtitle came from a conversation I had with a friend of mine, the poet and artist Annie Freud. She described how, on occasions when she woke in the early hours of the morning, feeling uneasy or disconsolate, she had often experienced the desire to reach for 'the right kind of poem'. Here is a book of poems intended to answer that need – poems that make space for the unexpected; offer an escape from the constant chatter of everyday thought and help us to reorient ourselves within the chaotic landscape of our lives. Some will delight; others may shock, move or unsettle you. Each one contains that element of surprise that can help shake us free of the confines of our own lives. Above all, this is a book for everyone; a book to carry around and to share, with friends, family and strangers – or, of course, to keep entirely for yourself, easily within reach on the bedside table.

All of the poems you'll find here have been included because I think they are excellent poems, and not because they happen to fit a predetermined theme. They are presented in five sections with each section suggesting a different way of looking at the world. This is very much a book to be dipped into at will, but if you are in a particular frame of mind, it may be that the poetry in one of the sections speaks to you more strongly at that time. Most of the poems here come from my own shelves – a collection built up over several decades that starts in bookcases and spills into loose rows propped against skirting boards. These are poems I love, poems I want to share, poems that have the power to excite and surprise me every time I return to them. But they are also poems that have been selected for their ability to console (though not necessarily to mollify: consolation comes in widely various forms and uses many slantwise tactics to achieve its aims). My hope is that you will discover your own favourites among them – poems you'll want to return to and have by heart.

Some critics have expressed disdain for what they see as the recent rise in popularity of anthologies that make a claim for the therapeutic value of words. Some have written with fondness of the old 'treasuries' that collected poems on their own merit, and not for their putative effect on readers' emotional well-being. But they are wrong to look to the past for corroboration of their views. The Victorians, for instance, were particularly amenable to the notion of poetry as consolation and produced a number of so-called therapeutic anthologies. The editor of one – *Poems of the Inner Life* (1872) – explains in his introduction that he has made his selection 'according to a sense of what most nearly touches the heart and mind in our best and most earnest hours'. The poems inside are arranged into sections headed 'Love', 'Prayer and Aspiration', 'Changes', 'Regrets', 'Longings' and so on. In other volumes the connection between poetry and medicine is more explicit: the masthead page of Schauffler's *The Poetry Cure: A Medicine Chest of Verse* (1925) flaunts an illustration of a pestle and mortar, and the contents are organised by malady – a whole section of 'Soothers and Soporifics', for instance, to aid the sleepless.

Presenting poems primarily as therapy in this way is perhaps extreme, and it runs the risk of eclipsing poetry's many other properties. Still, it remains true that poetry has strong curative powers, and there is no shortage of anecdotal evidence to prove it. Primo Levi – a chemist before he was a writer – assuaged the horrors of Auschwitz by reciting extracts from Dante's *Inferno* to a friend in the camp. He hadn't seen the poem since his school days but found he could remember long passages. Many years later he described how, amidst the hell of the concentration camp, the practice of reciting 'granted me a respite… in short, a way to find myself.'

In fact, the use of poetry as an aid to healing has a long and intriguing history, across cultures and across ages. Since early times, spiritual healers have chanted poetry for the well-being of the tribe. In ancient Egypt, patients drank word-infused water that had been poured over the lines of a healing spell inscribed on a stone slab, called a cippus. One of the earliest instances of the organised *reading* of poetry for health occurred in the second century BCE, when the physician Soranus prescribed poems for his mentally disturbed patients: comedy for depression and tragedy for mania. Not for nothing was Apollo given responsibility for both healing and poetry.

Fast forward several millennia to former *Times* columnist Rachel Kelly recounting the effects of learning and repeating lines from George Herbert's 'The Flower': 'In those moments of the day when I held hands with Herbert, the depression couldn't find me,' she explains. 'It felt as though the poet was embracing me from across the centuries... Here was a new and welcome voice in my head.' Nor are poets themselves immune to the therapeutic effects of poetry, though they may approach the idea with more resistance than most. Australian poet Les Murray found his attitude changing when he fell ill with depression: 'I'd disapproved of using poetry as personal therapy, but the Black Dog taught me better.'

How exactly do poems effect such a change in us? The medical profession has long been aware of the therapeutic value of poetry, but only recently has it started to study the process. It turns out that a poem's semantic content is only part of the story; the physical process of reading (or hearing) a poem also has a part to play. An investigation published in 2004 in the *American Journal of Physiology* focused on hexameter verse – the six-beat metre widely used in Classical times (the *Iliad* and the *Odyssey* are both written in hexameter).[1] Researchers examined the heart rates of healthy subjects while they recited lines of hexameter and for a short while afterwards, and came up with the same result time and again: reciting poetry synchronised the subjects' heart rates and breathing rates. As a result of their findings, the authors were able to advocate the use of poetry recitation for treating stress-related symptoms in the cardiorespiratory system.

Even more intriguingly, it has been shown that a line of metred poetry takes, on average, three seconds to recite, a fact that holds true across a wide range of languages – from ancient Greek to English to Japanese to Slavic. In 1983, poet Frederick Turner and neuroscientist Ernst Pöppel drew attention to the significance of this finding: they pointed out that the three-second reading time coincides with the length of what philosophers call the 'specious present' – the time it takes for the human brain to process the present moment. Because there are so many pieces of information in the world around us, entering the sensory cortex at different rates, around every three seconds, the cortex releases an information-bundle to the higher processing centres, and it's at that moment that we perceive the overall picture. It's similar to the way in which computers 'buffer' data when downloading video or audio content. Viewed this way, a poem may be said to be divided into a series of present moments, unfolding at the same rate at which we perceive our daily lives.[2]

As for the words themselves, the effects of a poem are never confined to its explainable content. Psychiatrist Smiley Blanton, who worked with Freud in the 1930s, described the 'electric charge' that went through him when he heard his great-uncle recite a Shakespeare sonnet. He felt the charge in spite of the fact that he was too young to understand, still less to relate to, the poem's content – proof, if it were needed, that the *sound* of a poem is central to the whole experience. Gerard Manley Hopkins knew this better than most: the music of his words brings 'The Windhover' (included here in the section titled 'Visible, Invisible') so vividly to life for us that it seems to lift from the page – a 'dapple-dawn-drawn Falcon, in his riding / Of the rolling level underneath him steady air'.

And *knowing* a poem – committing it to memory – can bring with it a raft of other benefits. In 2014, a team at the University of Cambridge established The Poetry and Memory Project, specifically to investigate the value of memorising poetry. 63 per cent of participants claimed their memorised poems brought comfort in tough times. It would seem that for many, a learned poem acts as a talisman or (as in Rachel Kelly's case) a companionable other – a distinctly separate, wiser being that walks alongside the reader. One participant in the Cambridge study remarked that certain poems had become 'like personal friends deeply rooted in my head'. Companionship is clearly an important part of the picture: whether in the depths of depression or not, the realisation that other people in other centuries were preoccupied with the same questions, hopes and anxieties as us can be hugely comforting.

Carrying a poem around in one's head can also sharpen our perceptions and lend intensity as we go about our daily business. When I see snow falling outside a window, it returns me to a window I know from a Louis MacNeice poem, 'Spawning snow and pink roses against it', and to a comment MacNeice makes in the poem about 'The drunkenness of things being various'. Because of the poem, a quite ordinary experience becomes something charged with meaning, enriched by my recollection of the words.

In the most affecting poems a transformation takes place – however gentle – both in the poem itself and within the reader. I believe that most people can gain from this most portable and memorable of art forms – not least because a poem's power to nudge us into a different level of awareness is a valuable antidote to the stasis of the human condition. A great poem dislodges something inside us; it effects a shift of perspective or consciousness.

Healing is, of course, only one of poetry's functions, and it is rarely the poet's primary aim. Poems come in many different shapes and forms – more so now in our computer-dominated age than ever – and they can serve almost as many ends. But attentive immersion in a great poem can be a life-changing – certainly a life-*enhancing* – experience. The healing properties of verse are limited, but they are also real. Smiley Blanton put it well in the introduction to *The Healing Power of Poetry* (1960), when he advised his readers that 'Poetry by itself will not cure you if you are suffering from a neurosis. But it will certainly make your neurosis easier to bear.'

Many of the poems in this volume may console, but the consolation they offer is far from anodyne. A deeper, and more lasting, comfort comes from art that makes us sit up and listen, that reawakens the senses and offers new ways of looking – poetry that, in the best sense, unsettles us, in order to reconnect us with the world around us and bring us to a place of greater clarity. The more open we are to that possibility, the more likely it is to happen. Emily Dickinson wrote that

'The soul should always stand ajar'; I hope readers of *Life Support* will keep that thought in mind as they dip into these pages.

Julia Copus
Somerset, 2019

A World in a Grain
of Sand

A World in a Grain
of Sand

Who hasn't at some time offered or received the advice
to put things into perspective, see things in context,
reconsider a problem 'in the grand scheme of things'?
The hope is that individual troubles will be dwarfed
when laid side by side with something bigger. There's
comfort, too, in remembering that the very concept of
size is relative, its parameters fluid enough to alter with
the context: a child's hand is huge and godlike when
viewed from the perspective of a goldfish, an immense
star tiny when reflected in a bucket of water.

In this section, we encounter worlds in which rock
pool barnacles are monks who 'sweep the broth as it
flows, with fans, / grooming every cubic millimetre'
and pine needles are perilously heavy (at least for an
ant setting out 'across the great, cloud-illuminated /

Sahara'). By the same token, even the beams of the sun are not so mighty that a lover lying late in bed with his sweetheart may not 'eclipse and cloud them with a winke'. As Emily Dickinson puts it, with her customary wisdom, 'The Brain – is wider than the Sky –'.

Shaking off the shackles of dimension can be thrillingly liberating. Andrew Young demonstrates how the world can be made new simply by raising a pair of binoculars to the eyes: in lifting the binoculars, says the speaker, 'I lift a field itself / as lightly as I might a shelf'. In fact human beings are naturally equipped to slip at will between perspectives of scale: the imagination will serve as well as any viewing apparatus, and has the advantage of being more portable.

The patient and meticulous miniaturists of Medieval times understood how much can be gained from paying attention to matters of scale and perspective. So too does the mother in Fleur Adcock's 'For a Five-Year Old' as she helps her child rescue a snail that has climbed into her bedroom after a night of rain. This mother knows by instinct – and in spite of her own failure to attend to such kindnesses – that in encouraging her child to focus on the small she is imparting one of the most valuable lessons there is to learn.

Daed-traa

I go to the rockpool at the slack of the tide
to mind me what my poetry's for.

It has its ventricles, just like us –
pumping brine, like bull's blood, a syrupy flow.

It has its theatre –
hushed and plush.

It has its Little Shop of Horrors.
It has its crossed and dotted monsters.

It has its cross-eyed beetling Lear.
It has its billowing Monroe.

I go to the rockpool at the slack of the tide
to mind me what my poetry's for.

For monks, it has barnacles
to sweep the broth as it flows, with fans,
grooming every cubic millimetre.

It has its ebb, the easy heft of wrack from rock,
like plastered, feverish locks of hair.

It has its *flodd*.
It has its welling god
with puddled, podgy cheeks and jaw.

It has its holy hiccup.

Its minute's silence

                     daed-traa.

I go to the rockpool at the slack of the tide
to mind me what my poetry's for.

    Jen Hadfield

Summer Farm

Straws like tame lightnings lie about the grass
And hang zigzag on hedges. Green as glass
The water in the horse-trough shines.
Nine ducks go wobbling by in two straight lines.

A hen stares at nothing with one eye,
Then picks it up. Out of an empty sky
A swallow falls and, flickering through
The barn, dives up again into the dizzy blue.

I lie, not thinking, in the cool, soft grass,
Afraid of where a thought might take me—as
This grasshopper with plated face
Unfolds his legs and finds himself in space.

Self under self, a pile of selves I stand
Threaded on time, and with metaphysic hand
Lift the farm like a lid and see
Farm within farm, and in the centre, me.

Norman MacCaig

For a Five-Year-Old

A snail is climbing up the window-sill
into your room, after a night of rain.
You call me in to see, and I explain
that it would be unkind to leave it there:
it might crawl to the floor; we must take care
that no one squashes it. You understand,
and carry it outside, with careful hand,
to eat a daffodil.

I see, then, that a kind of faith prevails:
your gentleness is moulded still by words
from me, who have trapped mice and shot wild birds,
from me, who drowned your kittens, who betrayed
your closest relatives, and who purveyed
the harshest kind of truth to many another.
But that is how things are: I am your mother,
and we are kind to snails.

Fleur Adcock

A Cranefly in September

She is struggling through grass-mesh—not flying,
Her wide-winged, stiff, weightless basket-work of
     limbs
Rocking, like an antique wain, a top-heavy ceremonial
     cart
Across mountain summits
(Not planing over water, dipping her tail)
But blundering with long strides, long reachings,
     reelings
And ginger-glistening wings
From collision to collision.
Aimless in no particular direction,
Just exerting her last to escape out of the
     overwhelming
Of whatever it is, legs, grass,
The garden, the county, the country, the world—

Sometimes she rests long minutes in the grass forest
Like a fairytale hero, only a marvel can help her.
She cannot fathom the mystery of this forest

In which, for instance, this giant watches—
The giant who knows she cannot be helped in any
    way.

Her jointed bamboo fuselage,
Her lobster shoulders, and her face
Like a pinhead dragon, with its tender moustache,
And the simple colourless church windows of her
    wings
Will come to an end, in mid-search, quite soon.
Everything about her, every perfected vestment
Is already superfluous.
The monstrous excess of her legs and curly feet
Are a problem beyond her.
The calculus of glucose and chitin inadequate
To plot her through the infinities of the stems.

Ted Hughes

'Tinily a star goes down'

Tinily a star goes down
behind a black cloud.

Odd that your wristwatch still should lie
on the shiny dressing table

its tick so faint I cannot hear
the universe at its centre.

Iain Crichton Smith

The Sunne Rising

Busie old foole, unruly Sunne,
        Why dost thou thus,
Through windowes, and through curtaines call on us?
Must to thy motions lovers seasons run?
        Sawcy pedantique wretch, goe chide
        Late schoole boyes, and sowre prentices,
    Goe tell Court-huntsmen, that the King will ride,
    Call countrey ants to harvest offices;
Love, all alike, no season knowes, nor clyme,
Nor houres, dayes, months, which are the rags of time.

        Thy beames, so reverend, and strong
        Why shouldst thou thinke?
I could eclipse and cloud them with a winke,
But that I would not lose her sight so long:
        If her eyes have not blinded thine,
        Looke, and to morrow late, tell mee,
    Whether both the'India's of spice and Myne
    Be where thou leftst them, or lie here with mee.
Aske for those Kings whom thou saw'st yesterday,
And thou shalt heare, All here in one bed lay.

She'is all States, and all Princes, I,
　　Nothing else is.
Princes doe but play us; compar'd to this,
All honor's mimique; All wealth alchimie.
　　Thou sunne art halfe as happy'as wee,
　　In that the world's contracted thus;
　Thine age askes ease, and since thy duties bee
　To warme the world, that's done in warming us.
Shine here to us, and thou art every where;
This bed thy center is, these walls, thy spheare.

John Donne

Zoom!

It begins as a house, an end terrace
in this case
    but it will not stop there. Soon it is
an avenue
    which cambers arrogantly past the Mechanics'
        Institute,
turns left
    at the main road without even looking
and quickly it is
    a town with all four major clearing banks,
a daily paper
    and a football team pushing for promotion.

On it goes, oblivious of the Planning Acts,
the green belts,
    and before we know it is out of our hands:
city, nation,
    hemisphere, universe, hammering out in all directions
until suddenly,
    mercifully, it is drawn aside through the eye
of a black hole

and bulleted into a neighbouring galaxy, emerging
smaller and smoother
    than a billiard ball but weighing more than Saturn.

People stop me in the street, badger me
in the check-out queue
    and ask 'What is this, this that is so small
and so very smooth
    but whose mass is greater than the ringed planet?'
It's just words
    I assure them. But they will not have it.

Simon Armitage

Of Many Worlds in this World

Just like as in a nest of boxes round,
Degrees of sizes in each box are found:
So, in this world, may many others be,
Thinner and less, and less still by degree:
Although they are not subject to our sense,
A world may be no bigger than two-pence.
Nature is curious, and such works may shape,
Which our dull senses easily escape:
For creatures, small as atoms, may be there,
If every one a creature's figure bear.
If atoms four, a world can make, then see
What several worlds might in an ear-ring be:
For millions of those atoms may be in
The head of one small, little, single pin.
And if thus small, then ladies may well wear
A world of worlds, as pendants in each ear.

Margaret Cavendish

Rubber

One pale morning in June at four o'clock
when the country roads were still gray and wet
in their endless tunnels of forest,
a car had passed over the clay
just where the ant came out busily with its pine needle
   now
and kept wandering around in the big G of "Goodyear"
that was imprinted in the sand of country roads
for a hundred and twenty kilometers.
Pine needles are heavy.
Time after time it slid back down with its tottering load
and worked its way up again
and slipped back again.
Outward bound across the great, cloud-illuminated
   Sahara.

Rolf Jacobsen
tr. Roger Greenwald

from *The Prelude*

It was a summer's night, a close warm night,
Wan, dull and glaring, with a dripping mist
Low-hung and thick that covered all the sky
Half threatening storm and rain; but on we went
Unchecked, being full of heart and having faith
In our tried pilot. Little could we see
Hemmed round on every side with fog and damp,
And, after ordinary travellers' chat
With our conductor, silently we sank
Each into commerce with his private thoughts.
Thus did we breast the ascent, and by myself
Was nothing either seen or heard the while
Which took me from my musings, save that once
The shepherd's cur did to his own great joy
Unearth a hedgehog in the mountain crags
Round which he made a barking turbulent.
This small adventure (for even such it seemed
In that wild place and at the dead of night)
Being over and forgotten, on we wound
In silence as before.
                        With forehead bent

Earthward, as if in opposition set
Against an enemy, I panted up
With eager pace, and no less eager thoughts.
Thus might we wear perhaps an hour away,
Ascending at loose distance each from each,
And I, as chanced, the foremost of the band –
When at my feet the ground appeared to brighten,
And with a step or two seemed brighter still;
Nor had I time to ask the cause of this,
For instantly a light upon the turf
Fell like a flash! I looked about, and lo,
The moon stood naked in the heavens at height
Immense above my head, and on the shore
I found myself of a huge sea of mist,
Which meek and silent rested at my feet.
A hundred hills their dusky backs upheaved
All over this still ocean; and beyond,
Far, far beyond, the vapours shot themselves
In headlands, tongues, and promontory shapes,
Into the sea – the real sea, that seemed
To dwindle and give up its majesty,

Usurped upon as far as sight could reach.
Meanwhile, the moon looked down upon this show
In single glory, and we stood, the mist
Touching our very feet. And from the shore
At distance not the third part of a mile
Was a blue chasm, a fracture in the vapour,
A deep and gloomy breathing-place through which
Mounted the roar of waters, torrents, streams
Innumerable, roaring with one voice!
The universal spectacle throughout
Was shaped for admiration and delight,
Grand in itself alone, but in that breach
Through which the homeless voice of waters rose,
That dark deep thoroughfare, had nature lodged
The soul, the imagination of the whole.

William Wordsworth

Blossom

There's this life and no hereafter –
                I'm sure of that
but still I dither, waiting
for my laggard soul
to leap at the world's touch.

How many May dawns
              have I slept right through,
the trees courageous with blossom?
Let me number them...

I shall be weighed in the balance
                and found wanting.
I shall reckon for less
              than an apple pip.

Kathleen Jamie

Words, Wide Night

Somewhere, on the other side of this wide night
and the distance between us, I am thinking of you.
The room is turning slowly away from the moon.

This is pleasurable. Or shall I cross that out and say
it is sad? In one of the tenses I singing
an impossible song of desire that you cannot hear.

La lala la. See? I close my eyes and imagine
the dark hills I would have to cross
to reach you. For I am in love with you and this

is what it is like or what it is like in words.

Carol Ann Duffy

Being a Wife

So this is what it's like being a wife.
The body I remember feeling as big as America in,
the thighs so far away
his hand had to ride in an aeroplane to get there;
the giggles I heard adults giggling with
I was puzzled about,
and felt much too solemn to try;
buttons unbuttoned by somebody else, not me;
the record-player
neither of us were able to stop what we were doing
to turn off;
the smell of fish
I dreaded I'd never get used to,
the peculiar, leering, antediluvian taste
I preferred not to taste;
the feeling of being on the edge of something
everyone older than us,
had wasted,
and not understood,
as we were about to do;
his pink hand gripping my breast

as if his life depended on it;
the shame of the thought of the mirror
reflecting all this,
seem long ago,
yet somehow authentic and right.
Being a wife is like acting being a wife,
and the me that was her with him in the past is still me.

Selima Hill

'The Brain — is wider than the Sky —'

The Brain — is wider than the Sky —
For — put them side by side —
The one the other will contain
With ease — and You — beside —

The Brain is deeper than the sea —
For — hold them — Blue to Blue —
The one the other will absorb —
As Sponges — Buckets — do —

The Brain is just the weight of God —
For — Heft them — Pound for Pound
And they will differ — if they do —
As Syllable from Sound —

Emily Dickinson

Stargazing

The night is fine and dry. It falls and spreads
the cold sky with a million opposites
that, for a moment, seem like a million souls
and soon, none, and then, for what seems a long time,
one. Then of course it spins. What is better to do
than string out over the infinite dead spaces
the ancient beasts and spearmen of the human
mind, and, if not the real ones, new ones?

But, try making them clear to one you love –
whoever is standing by you is one you love
when pinioned by the stars – you will find it quite
impossible, but like her more for thinking
she sees that constellation.

After the wave of pain, you will turn to her
and, in an instant, change the universe
to a sky you were glad you came outside to see.
This is the act of all the descended gods
of every age and creed: to weary of all

that never ends, to take a human hand,
and go back into the house.

Glyn Maxwell

Field-Glasses

Though buds still speak in hints
And frozen ground has set the flints
As fast as precious stones
And birds perch on the boughs, silent as cones.

Suddenly waked from sloth
Young trees put on a ten years' growth
And stones double their size,
Drawn nearer through field-glasses' greater eyes.

Why I borrow their sight
Is not to give small birds a fright
Creeping up close by inches;
I make the trees come, bringing tits and finches.

I lift a field itself
As lightly as I might a shelf,
And the rooks do not rage
Caught for a moment in my crystal cage.

And while I stand and look,
Their private lives an open book,
I feel so privileged
My shoulders prick, as though they were half-fledged.

Andrew Young

Full Moon and Little Frieda

A cool small evening shrunk to a dog bark and the
     clank of a bucket –

And you listening.
A spider's web, tense for the dew's touch.
A pail lifted, still and brimming – mirror
To tempt a first star to a tremor.

Cows are going home in the lane there, looping the
     hedges with their warm wreaths of breath –
A dark river of blood, many boulders,
Balancing unspilled milk.

'Moon!' you cry suddenly, 'Moon! Moon!'

The moon has stepped back like an artist gazing
     amazed at a work

That points at him amazed.

Ted Hughes

Another Self

Another Self

Over two thousand years ago, in his treatise 'On Friendship', Cicero suggested that the *verus amicus*, or true friend, was essentially another self. It was a notion he had inherited from Aristotle, and it's one that many of us have experienced – the sense of kinship that binds us so strongly to another that they become a part of us, and we of them; a kind of Venn diagram of souls. The Greeks named the sensation *philia*, and it underpins all of the poems in this group.

Here you will find siblings, lovers, spouses, parents, drinking partners, friends and more. Many of the poems are addressed directly to the second self. Some of those selves are in different locations, some belong to the past, some to the future, and a few are no longer living, but in every case the connection itself survives the absence; it continues to provide sustenance and comfort for the poem's speaker.

Romantic love is perhaps the most obvious condition in which we may feel ourselves bound to a second self, but there are many other ways: the bond may come from a shared anonymity with a stranger (as in Emily Dickinson's 'I'm nobody! Who are you?'), through shared sleep, a common history, the anticipation of times to come or the contemplation of union in death. Our awareness of such bonds is often occasioned by an unexpected event – by the need to 'look about and find a sheltering place', as happens in John Clare's 'Sudden Shower'. It follows that the greater the crisis – and therefore the more vulnerable we are – the greater the sense of connection we experience. And such connections may remain even when the danger comes from within: in Selima Hill's 'Nuage Argente', a couple is united by the havoc one partner is wreaking on their relationship. The poem ends with one of the tenderest moments I know of in poetry, in which the speaker equates her persistent prayers for help with the action of a farmer running their hands through grain 'to coax large animals to come to them'.

W. S. Graham's 'Lines on Roger Hilton's Watch' is evidence of the deep, sustaining value of friendship in hard times. Graham and Hilton (a painter) were drinking partners, and the poem begins and ends with the assertion that the two men had 'terrible times together'. Further testimony comes from Rebecca Perry's 'Soup Sister' who asks 'How did we always manage / to be heartbroken at the same time?' In the absence of her soulmate, the speaker is reminded of her friend by a certain tree she passes on a walk, a tree that has 'a kind look and tiny sub-branches / like your delicate wrists'. The instinct to draw closer in the midst of life's difficulties stems from an ancient survival mechanism; the poems here remind us that sharing such times can lead to the deepest of human bonds.

Crossing the Loch

Remember how we rowed toward the cottage
on the sickle-shaped bay,
that one night after the pub
loosed us through its swinging doors
and we pushed across the shingle
till water lipped the sides
as though the loch mouthed 'boat'?

I forget who rowed. Our jokes hushed.
The oars' splash, creak, and the spill
of the loch reached long into the night.
Out in the race I was scared:
the cold shawl of breeze,
and hunched hills; what the water held
of deadheads, ticking nuclear hulls.

Who rowed, and who kept their peace?
Who hauled salt-air and stars
deep into their lungs, were not reassured;
and who first noticed the loch's
phosphorescence, so, like a twittering nest

washed from the rushes, an astonished
small boat of saints, we watched water shine
on our fingers and oars,
the magic dart of our bow wave?

It was surely foolhardy, such a broad loch, a tide,
but we live – and even have children
to women and men we had yet to meet
that night we set out, calling our own
the sky and salt-water, wounded hills
dark-starred by blaeberries, the glimmering anklets
we wore in the shallows
as we shipped oars and jumped,
to draw the boat safe, high at the cottage shore.

Kathleen Jamie

Lines on Roger Hilton's Watch

Which I was given because
I loved him and we had
Terrible times together.

O tarnished ticking time
Piece with your bent hand,
You must be used to being

Looked at suddenly
In the middle of the night
When he switched the light on
Beside his bed. I hope
You told him the best time
When he lifted you up
To meet the Hilton gaze.

I lift you up from the mantel
Piece here in my house
Wearing your verdigris.
At least I keep you wound

And put my ear to you
To hear Botallack tick.

You realise your master
Has relinquished you
And gone to lie under
The ground at St Just.

Tell me the time. The time
Is Botallack o'clock.
This is the dead of night.

   He switches the light on
   To find a cigarette
   And pours himself a Teachers.
   He picks me up and holds me
   Near his lonely face
   To see my hands. He thinks
   He is not being watched.

The images of his dream
Are still about his face
As he spits and tries not
To remember where he was.

I am only a watch
And pray time hastes away.
I think I am running down.

Watch, it is time I wound
You up again. I am
Very much not your dear
Last master but we had
Terrible times together.

W. S. Graham

Sonnet 104

To me, fair friend, you never can be old,
For as you were when first your eye I eyed,
Such seems your beauty still. Three winters cold
Have from the forests shook three summers' pride,
Three beauteous springs to yellow autumn turned
In process of the seasons have I seen,
Three April perfumes in three hot Junes burned,
Since first I saw you fresh, which yet are green.
Ah, yet doth beauty, like a dial hand,
Steal from his figure, and no pace perceived;
So your sweet hue, which methinks still doth stand,
Hath motion, and mine eye may be deceived;
  For fear of which, hear this, thou age unbred:
  Ere you were born was beauty's summer dead.

William Shakespeare

Taking the Hands

Taking the hands of someone you love,
You see they are delicate cages...
Tiny birds are singing
In the secluded prairies
And in the deep valleys of the hand.

Robert Bly

Nuage Argente

Nuage Argente –
the name of the house
you betrayed us in,
sucking each other to bits
like two chunks of chopped fish
made fat from feeding on the blood and tears
of other people's partners
and your own.
What a noise
you must be making
behind the curtains
in the little room.
You sometimes soak the sheets.
You sometimes lie.
You 'can't believe you did this'.
Nor can I.
Every day I'll dip you in my syrup.
I'll dip you in and force you to be lovable
and roll you around
in trays of hundreds and thousands.
The lowest of the low my mother called them,

men who messed with other people's wives.
Today's today.
It will not come again.
Somewhere in your heart
there must be tenderness.
If you've got one.
Which they say you have.
You know how farmers
run their hands through grain
to coax large animals to come to them?
I'm running my words
through buckets of prayers like that
to coax something out of the dark
to come and save us.

Selima Hill

At Night

In the dust are my father's beautiful hands,
In the dust are my mother's eyes.
Here by the shore of the ocean standing,
Watching: still I do not understand.

Love flows over me, around me,
Here at night by the sea, by the sovereign sea.

Gone is that bone-hoard of strength;
Gone her gentle motion laughing, walking.

Is it not strange that disease and death
Should rest, by the undulant sea?

And I stare, rich with gifts, alone.

Feeling from the sea those terrene presences,
My father's hands, my mother's eyes.

Richard Eberhart

'I'm nobody! Who are you?'

I'm nobody! Who are you?
Are you nobody, too?
Then there's a pair of us—don't tell!
They'd banish us, you know.

How dreary to be somebody!
How public, like a frog
To tell your name the livelong day
To an admiring bog!

Emily Dickinson

I shall be released

What we love
   will leave us

or is it
   we leave

what we love,
   I forget—

Today, belly
   full enough

to walk the block
   after all week

too cold
   outside to smile—

I think of you, warm
   in your underground room

reading the book
   of bone. It's hard going—

your body a dead
   language—

I've begun
   to feel, if not

hope then what
   comes just after—

or before—
   Let's not call it

regret, but
   this weight,

or weightlessness,
   or just

plain waiting.
   The ice wanting

again water.
   The streams of two planes

a cross fading.

I was so busy
   telling you this I forgot

to mention the sky—
   how in the dusk

its steely edges
   have just begun to rust.

   Kevin Young

Meeting at Night

The gray sea and the long black land;
And the yellow half-moon large and low;
And the startled little waves that leap
In fiery ringlets from their sleep,
As I gain the cove with pushing prow,
And quench its speed i' the slushy sand.

Then a mile of warm sea-scented beach;
Three fields to cross till a farm appears;
A tap at the pane, the quick sharp scratch
And blue spurt of a lighted match,
And a voice less loud, thro' its joys and fears,
Than the two hearts beating each to each!

Robert Browning

Sudden Shower

Black grows the southern sky betokening rain
And humming hive-bees homeward hurry by;
They feel the change—so let us shun the grain
And take the broad road while our feet are dry.
Ay, there some dropples moistened in my face
And pattered on my hat—'tis coming nigh—
Let's look about and find a sheltering place.
The little things around, like you and I,
Are hurrying through the grass to shun the shower.
Here stoops an ash tree—hark, the wind gets high,
But never mind, this ivy for an hour,
Rain as it may, will keep us dryly here.
That little wren knows well his sheltering bower
Nor leaves his dry house though we come so near.

John Clare

Soup Sister

And, of course,
it bothers me greatly that I can't know
the quality of the light where you are.
How your each day pans out,
how the breeze lifts the dry leaves from the street
or how the street pulls away from the rain.

Last week I passed a tree
that was exactly you in tree form,
with a kind look and tiny sub-branches
like your delicate wrists.

Six years ago we were lying
in a dark front room on perpendicular sofas,
so hungover that our skin hurt to touch.
How did we always manage
to be heartbroken at the same time?

I could chop, de-seed and roast
a butternut squash for dinner
in the time it took you to shower.

Steam curtained the windows, whiting out
the rain, which hit the house sideways.
One of us, though I forget who, said
do you think women are treated like bowls
waiting to be filled with soup?
And the other one said, of course.

Now the world is too big,
and it's sinking and rising
and stretching out its back bones,
The rivers are too wild,
the mountains are so so old
and it's all laid out arrogantly between us.

My friend, how long do you stand
staring at the socks in your drawer
lined up neat as buns in a bakery,
losing track of time and your place in the world,
in the (custardy light of a) morning?

Rebecca Perry

'As our bloods separate'

As our bloods separate the clock resumes,
I hear the wind again as our hearts quieten.
We were a ring: the clock ticked round us
For that time and the wind was deflected.

The clock pecks everything to the bone.
The wind enters through the broken eyes
Of houses and through their wide mouths
And scatters the ashes from the hearth.

Sleep. Do not let go my hand.

David Constantine

The Bracelet: To Julia

Why I tie about thy wrist,
Julia, this silken twist;
For what other reason is't
But to show thee how, in part,
Thou my pretty captive art?
But thy bond-slave is my heart:
'Tis but silk that bindeth thee,
Knap the thread and thou art free;
But 'tis otherwise with me:
—I am bound and fast bound, so
That from thee I cannot go;
If I could, I would not so.

Robert Herrick

The sun used to shine

The sun used to shine while we two walked
Slowly together, paused and started
Again, and sometimes mused, sometimes talked
As either pleased, and cheerfully parted

Each night. We never disagreed
Which gate to rest on. The to be
And the late past we gave small heed.
We turned from men or poetry

To rumours of the war remote
Only till both stood disinclined
For aught but the yellow flavorous coat
Of an apple wasps had undermined;

Or a sentry of dark betonies,
The stateliest of small flowers on earth,
At the forest verge; or crocuses
Pale purple as if they had their birth

In sunless Hades fields. The war
Came back to mind with the moonrise
Which soldiers in the east afar
Beheld then. Nevertheless, our eyes

Could as well imagine the Crusades
Or Caesar's battles. Everything
To faintness like those rumours fades –
Like the brook's water glittering

Under the moonlight – like those walks
Now – like us two that took them, and
The fallen apples, all the talks
And silences – like memory's sand

When the tide covers it late or soon,
And other men through other flowers
In those fields under the same moon
Go talking and have easy hours.

Edward Thomas

Love

Love bade me welcome; yet my soul drew back,
     Guilty of dust and sin.
But quick-eyed Love, observing me grow slack
     From my first entrance in,
Drew nearer to me, sweetly questioning
     If I lack'd anything.

'A guest,' I answer'd, 'worthy to be here:'
     Love said, 'You shall be he.'
'I, the unkind, ungrateful? Ah, my dear,
     I cannot look on Thee.'
Love took my hand and smiling did reply,
     'Who made the eyes but I?'

'Truth, Lord; but I have marr'd them: let my shame
     Go where it doth deserve.'
'And know you not,' says Love, 'Who bore the blame?'
     'My dear, then I will serve.'
'You must sit down,' says Love, 'and taste my meat.'
     So I did sit and eat.

George Herbert

Summer Nocturne

Let us love this distance, since those who do not love
each other are not separated.
—Simone Weil

Night without you, and the dog barking at the silence,
no doubt at what's *in* the silence,
a deer perhaps pruning the rhododendron
or that raccoon with its brilliant fingers
testing the garbage can lid by the shed.

Night I've chosen a book to help me think
about the long that's in longing, "the space across
which desire reaches." Night that finally needs music
to quiet the dog and whatever enormous animal
night itself is, appetite without limit.

Since I seem to want to be hurt a little,
it's Stan Getz and "It Never Entered My Mind,"
and to back him up Johnnie Walker Black
coming down now from the cabinet to sing
of its twelve lonely years in the dark.

Night of small revelations, night of odd comfort.
Starting to love this distance.
Starting to feel how present you are in it.

Stephen Dunn

The Hug

It was your birthday, we had drunk and dined
   Half of the night with our old friend.
     Who'd showed us in the end
   To a bed I reached in one drunk stride.
     Already I lay snug,
And drowsy with the wine dozed on one side.

I dozed, I slept. My sleep broke on a hug,
     Suddenly, from behind,
In which the full lengths of our bodies pressed:
     Your instep to my heel,
   My shoulder-blades against your chest.
   It was not sex, but I could feel
   The whole strength of your body set,
     Or braced, to mine,
     And locking me to you
   As if we were still twenty-two
   When our grand passion had not yet
     Become familial.
   My quick sleep had deleted all
   Of intervening time and place.

I only knew
The stay of your secure firm dry embrace.

Thom Gunn

Animals

Have you forgotten what we were like then
when we were still first rate
and the day came fat with an apple in its mouth

it's no use worrying about Time
but we did have a few tricks up our sleeves
and turned some sharp corners

the whole pasture looked like our meal
we didn't need speedometers
we could manage cocktails out of ice and water

I wouldn't want to be faster
or greener than now if you were with me O you
were the best of all my days

Frank O'Hara

Sunlight

for Mary Heaney

(*from* Mossbawn: Two Poems in Dedication)

There was a sunlit absence.
The helmeted pump in the yard
heated its iron,
water honeyed

in the slung bucket
and the sun stood
like a griddle cooling
against the wall

of each long afternoon.
So, her hands scuffled
over the bakeboard,
the reddening stove

sent its plaque of heat
against her where she stood
in a floury apron
by the window.

Now she dusts the board
with a goose's wing,
now sits, broad-lapped,
with whitened nails

and measling shins:
here is a space
again, the scone rising
to the tick of two clocks.

And here is love
like a tinsmith's scoop
sunk past its gleam
in the meal-bin.

Seamus Heaney

And for That Minute
a Blackbird Sang

And for That Minute
a Blackbird Sang

The ancient Greeks had two words for time: the sort of time that is ticked away by the second-hand of our modern clocks was called *chronos*. But *kairos* is something different altogether. *Kairos* exists outside the confines of space-time, unmeasured and unmeasurable. It defines time in which something exceptional – maybe even life-changing – takes place. We see our first snowfall, climb mountains and fall in love in *kairos* time. But we can also experience it on more mundane occasions.

Edward Thomas's train journey through Adlestrop is a perfect example, containing as it does an apparently ordinary moment in which his train pauses at the station ('The steam hissed. Someone cleared his throat.'). And yet the speaker feels the moment to be teeming with life. All the poems you'll encounter here describe a similar sensation – awareness of 'the moment eternal', as Browning calls it. The settings and circumstances, though, are widely varied: a man shares a coke with his lover in 'the warm New York 4 o'clock light'; a father watches his son walk away from him after a football match in favour of joining his friends; a young woman in mid-summer, her skin 'peppery with sweat' from a long bus journey, catches a first glimpse of her boyfriend. And in Jean Sprackland's 'Hands', a mother standing idly in the 'steam and banter' of a fish and chip shop is transported to a memory of her son's birth. These are moments of heightened awareness, when the small events in our lives become loaded with meaning.

In modern Greek, *kairos* means 'weather' rather than time – an indication, perhaps, that time is less a quantifiable substance than a state of mind. Experiences of the kind portrayed here suggest that the richness of our lives is determined not so much by what those lives contain as by the quality of our perception, from moment to moment – a fact to which all the characters in this section bear witness, from the builder on a rooftop, kneeling upright to rest his back, to the lone diner diverted by a childhood memory as he sits down to his pot roast. Knowing this, we might all benefit from paying heed to the passenger in Robert Creeley's playful 'I Know a

Man', as he reminds the endlessly philosophising driver to 'look / out where yr going'.

Over the centuries, we human beings have used all sorts of means to regulate the passage of time – sunlight, water, sand, wax, oil, quartz, satellites – with the intention of imposing order on the world around us. But it's not impossible to envisage a world in which *kairos* time dominates, a world where time exists primarily as a quality. (Clocks are, after all, no more than witnesses of time; mere bystanders.) I imagine living a life this way would feel a little like building a monument – a stockpile of meaningful moments heaped up like a cairn – to be revisited and viewed in quieter times. And if the moments were to be set in motion again, each one would run at its original pace, powered by the emotion that formed it. That is precisely what happens in Robert Browning's 'Now', a sonnet that fixes on a single moment of intimacy with such force that the experience endures: 'You around me for once, you beneath me, above me'. Here is a collection of many such moments – each one undamaged by the passing of ordinary time, existing, as it does, forever outside it.

Everything Is Going To Be All Right

How should I not be glad to contemplate
the clouds clearing beyond the dormer window
and a high tide reflected on the ceiling?
There will be dying, there will be dying,
but there is no need to go into that.
The poems flow from the hand unbidden
and the hidden source is the watchful heart.
The sun rises in spite of everything
and the far cities are beautiful and bright.
I lie here in a riot of sunlight
watching the day break and the clouds flying.
Everything is going to be all right.

Derek Mahon

A Hill

In Italy, where this sort of thing can occur,
I had a vision once – though you understand
It was nothing at all like Dante's, or the visions of
    saints.
And perhaps not a vision at all. I was with some
    friends.
Picking my way through a warm sunlit piazza
In the early morning. A clear fretwork of shadows
From huge umbrellas littered the pavement and made
A sort of lucent shallows in which was moored
A small navy of carts. Books, coins, old maps,
Cheap landscapes and ugly religious prints
Were all on sale. The colors and noise
Like the flying hands were gestures of exultation,
So that even the bargaining
Rose to the ear like a voluble godliness.
And then, where it happened, the noises suddenly
    stopped,
And it got darker; pushcarts and people dissolved
And even the great Farnese Palace itself
Was gone, for all its marble; in its place

Was a hill, mole-colored and bare. It was very cold,
Close to freezing, with a promise of snow.
The trees were like old ironwork gathered for scrap
Outside a factory wall. There was no wind,
And the only sound for a while was the little click
Of ice as it broke in the mud under my feet.
I saw a piece of ribbon snagged on a hedge,
But no other sign of life. And then I heard
What seemed the crack of a rifle. A hunter, I guessed;
At least I was not alone. But just after that
Came the soft and papery crash
Of a great branch somewhere unseen falling to earth.

And that was all, except for the cold and silence
That promised to last forever, like the hill.

Then prices came through, and fingers, and I was
    restored
To the sunlight and my friends. But for more than a
    week
I was scared by the plain bitterness of what I had seen.

All this happened about ten years ago.
And it hasn't troubled me since, but at last, today,
I remembered that hill; it lies just to the left
Of the road north of Poughkeepsie; and as a boy
I stood before it for hours in wintertime.

Anthony Hecht

Prelude I

The winter evening settles down
With smell of steaks in passageways.
Six o'clock.
The burnt-out ends of smoky days.
And now a gusty shower wraps
The grimy scraps
Of withered leaves about your feet
And newspapers from vacant lots;
The showers beat
On broken blinds and chimney-pots,
And at the corner of the street
A lonely cab-horse steams and stamps.

And then the lighting of the lamps.

T. S. Eliot

Hands

She peels cod fillets off the slab,
dips them in batter, drops them
one by one into the storm of hot fat.
I watch her scrubbed hands,
elegant at the work

and think of the hands of the midwife
stroking wet hair from my face as I sobbed and cursed,
calling me Sweetheart and wheeling in more gas,
hauling out at last my slippery fish of a son.
He was all silence and milky blue. She took him away
and brought him back breathing,
wrapped in a white sheet. By then
I loved her like my own mother.

I stand here speechless in the steam and banter,
as she makes hospital corners of my hot paper parcel.

Jean Sprackland

Now

Out of your whole life give but a moment!
All of your life that has gone before,
All to come after it, – so you ignore,
So you make perfect the present, – condense,
In a rapture of rage, for perfection's endowment,
Thought and feeling and soul and sense –
Merged in a moment which gives me at last
You around me for once, you beneath me, above me –
Me – sure that despite of time future, time past, –
This tick of our life-time's one moment you love me!
How long such suspension may linger? Ah, Sweet –
The moment eternal – just that and no more –
When ecstasy's utmost we clutch at the core
While cheeks burn, arms open, eyes shut and lips meet!

Robert Browning

Still-Life

Through the open French window the warm sun
lights up the polished breakfast-table, laid
round a bowl of crimson roses, for one –
a service of Worcester porcelain, arrayed
near it a melon, peaches, figs, small hot
rolls in a napkin, fairy rack of toast,
butter in ice, high silver coffee-pot,
and, heaped on a salver, the morning's post.

She comes over the lawn, the young heiress,
from her early walk in her garden-wood
feeling that life's a table set to bless
her delicate desires with all that's good,

that even the unopened future lies
like a love-letter, full of sweet surprise.

Elizabeth Daryush

Poem for James

Summer; thunder pulsed on the horizon
while hummingbirds slipped through the thickened air
to circle the dropper, sip sugared water,
and I half-waded, half-swam, thigh-deep in pollen,
which rose in a haze from their meadow-grown lawn.
I was straight off the bus in that glaze of heat,
my unwashed skin peppery with sweat,
rucksack, camera, dirt, bearing me down
to the devil. But there you were, waist-deep in saffron,
your long arms folded and every hair on them
glowing like bronze, your red hair on fire
and your dark eyes attentive, though you don't
    remember,
which is why I'm writing it down, from the goldenrod
    in bloom
to your nimbus of insects lit by the sun.

Fiona Benson

The Solitary Reaper

Behold her, single in the field,
Yon solitary Highland Lass!
Reaping and singing by herself;
Stop here, or gently pass!
Alone she cuts and binds the grain,
And sings a melancholy strain;
O listen! for the Vale profound
Is overflowing with the sound.

No Nightingale did ever chaunt
More welcome notes to weary bands
Of travellers in some shady haunt,
Among Arabian sands:
A voice so thrilling ne'er was heard
In spring-time from the Cuckoo-bird,
Breaking the silence of the seas
Among the farthest Hebrides.

Will no one tell me what she sings? –
Perhaps the plaintive numbers flow
For old, unhappy, far-off things,

And battles long ago:
Or is it some more humble lay,
Familiar matter of today?
Some natural sorrow, loss, or pain,
That has been, and may be again?

Whate'er the theme, the Maiden sang
As if her song could have no ending;
saw her singing at her work,
And o'er the sickle bending; –
I listened, motionless and still;
And, as I mounted up the hill,
The music in my heart I bore,
Long after it was heard no more.

William Wordsworth

Walking Away

for Sean

It is eighteen years ago, almost to the day –
A sunny day with the leaves just turning,
The touch-lines new-ruled – since I watched you play
Your first game of football, then, like a satellite
Wrenched from its orbit, go drifting away

Behind a scatter of boys. I can see
You walking away from me towards the school
With the pathos of a half-fledged thing set free
Into a wilderness, the gait of one
Who finds no path where the path should be.

That hesitant figure, eddying away
Like a winged seed loosened from its parent stem
Has something I never quite grasp to convey
About nature's give-and-take – the small, the scorching
Ordeals which fire one's irresolute clay.

I have had worse partings, but none that so
Gnaws at my mind still. Perhaps it is roughly
Saying what God alone could perfectly show –

How selfhood begins with a walking away,
And love is proved in the letting go.

C. Day Lewis

Cycle

As she proffered
that enormous gin and tonic,
the clink of ice-cubes jostling
brought to mind
an amphitheatre
scooped from a sun-lulled hillside,
where a small breeze carried
the scent of lemon-trees
and distant jostle of goat-bells,
bringing to mind
an enormous gin and tonic.

Christopher Reid

Autumn

A touch of cold in the Autumn night –
I walked abroad,
And saw the ruddy moon lean over a hedge
Like a red-faced farmer.
I did not stop to speak, but nodded,
And round about were the wistful stars
With white faces like town children.

T. E. Hulme

Adlestrop

Yes. I remember Adlestrop –
The name, because one afternoon
Of heat the express-train drew up there
Unwontedly. It was late June.

The steam hissed. Someone cleared his throat.
No one left and no one came
On the bare platform. What I saw
Was Adlestrop – only the name

And willows, willow-herb, and grass,
And meadowsweet, and haycocks dry,
No whit less still and lonely fair
Than the high cloudlets in the sky.

And for that minute a blackbird sang
Close by, and round him, mistier,
Farther and farther, all the birds
Of Oxfordshire and Gloucestershire.

Edward Thomas

Pot Roast

I gaze upon the roast,
that is sliced and laid out
on my plate,
and over it
I spoon the juices
of carrot and onion.
And for once I do not regret
the passage of time.

I sit by a window
that looks
on the soot-stained brick of buildings
and do not care that I see
no living thing—not a bird,
not a branch in bloom,
not a soul moving
in the rooms
behind the dark panes.
These days when there is little
to love or to praise
one could do worse

than yield
to the power of food.
So I bend

to inhale
the steam that rises
from my plate, and I think
of the first time
I tasted a roast
like this.
It was years ago
in Seabright,
Nova Scotia;
my mother leaned
over my dish and filled it
and when I finished
filled it again.
I remember the gravy,
its odor of garlic and celery,
and sopping it up
with pieces of bread.

And now
I taste it again.
The meat of memory.
The meat of no change.
I raise my fork
and I eat.

Mark Strand

'After dark vapours have oppressed
our plains'

After dark vapours have oppressed our plains
 For a long dreary season, comes a day
 Born of the gentle South, and clears away
From the sick heavens all unseemly stains.
The anxious month, relieving from its pains,
 Takes as a long-lost right the feel of May,
 The eyelids with the passing coolness play,
Like rose leaves with the drip of summer rains.
And calmest thoughts come round us – as of leaves
 Budding – fruit ripening in stillness – autumn suns
Smiling at eve upon the quiet sheaves –
Sweet Sappho's cheek – a sleeping infant's breath –
 The gradual sand that through an hour-glass runs –
A woodland rivulet – a Poet's death.

John Keats

Behaviour of Fish in an Egyptian Tea Garden

As a white stone draws down the fish
she on the seafloor of the afternoon
draws down men's glances and their cruel wish
for love. Slyly red lip on the spoon

slips in a morsel of ice-cream; her hands
white as a milky stone; white submarine
fronds, sink with spread fingers, lean
along the table, carmined at the ends.

A cotton magnate, an important fish
with great eyepouches and a golden mouth
through the frail reefs of furniture swims out
and idling, suspended, stays to watch.

A crustacean old man clamped to his chair
sits coldly near her and might see
her charms through fissures where the eyes should be
or else his teeth are parted in a stare.

Captain on leave, a lean dark mackerel,
lies in the offing; turns himself and looks
through currents of sound. The flat-eyed flatfish sucks
on a straw, staring from its repose, laxly.

And gallants in shoals swim up and lag,
circling and passing near the white attraction:
sometimes pausing, opening a conversation;
fish pause so to nibble or tug.

Now the ice-cream is finished, is
paid for. The fish swim off on business
and she sits alone at the table, a white stone
useless except to a collector, a rich man.

Keith Douglas

I Know a Man

As I sd to my
friend, because I am
always talking, – John, I

sd, which was not his
name, the darkness sur-
rounds us, what

can we do against
it, or else, shall we &
why not, buy a goddamn big car,

drive, he sd, for
christ's sake, look
out where yr going.

Robert Creeley

A Thunderstorm in Town

(A Reminiscence: 1893)

She wore a new 'terra-cotta' dress,
And we stayed, because of the pelting storm,
Within the hansom's dry recess,
Though the horse had stopped; yea, motionless
    We sat on, snug and warm.

Then the downpour ceased, to my sharp sad pain,
And the glass that had screened our forms before
Flew up, and out she sprang to her door:
I should have kissed her if the rain
    Had lasted a minute more.

Thomas Hardy

Ivan

Our rooster's name is Ivan.
He rules the world.
He stands on a bucket to assist
the sun in its path
through the sky. He
will not be attending
the funeral, for God

has said to Ivan, *You*
will never be sick
or senile. I'll
kill you with lightning
or let you drown. Or

I'll simply send
an eagle down
to fetch you when you're done.

So Ivan stands on a bucket
and looks around:

Human
stupidity.
The pitiful
cornflakes in their bowls.
The statues of their fascists.
The insane division of their cells.
The misinterpretations
of their bibles. Their
homely combs—and,
today, absurdly, their
crisp black clothes.

But Ivan keeps his thoughts
to himself, and crows.

Laura Kasischke

Snow

The room was suddenly rich and the great
   bay-window was
Spawning snow and pink roses against it
Soundlessly collateral and incompatible:
World is suddener than we fancy it.

World is crazier and more of it than we think.
Incorrigibly plural. I peel and portion
A tangerine and spit the pips and feel
The drunkenness of things being various.

And the fire flames with a bubbling sound for world
Is more spiteful and gay than one supposes —
On the tongue on the eyes on the ears in the palms of
   one's hands —
There is more than glass between the snow and the
   huge roses.

Louis MacNeice

Composed upon Westminster Bridge

Sept. 3, 1802

Earth has not any thing to shew more fair:
Dull would he be of soul who could pass by
A sight so touching in its majesty:
This City now doth like a garment wear
The beauty of the morning; silent, bare,
Ships, towers, domes, theatres, and temples lie
Open unto the fields, and to the sky;
All bright and glittering in the smokeless air.
Never did sun more beautifully steep
In his first splendor valley, rock, or hill;
Ne'er saw I, never felt, a calm so deep!
The river glideth at his own sweet will:
Dear God! the very houses seem asleep;
And all that mighty heart is lying still!

William Wordsworth

Having a Coke with You

is even more fun than going to San Sebastian, Irún,
  Hendaye, Biarritz, Bayonne
or being sick to my stomach on the Travesera de
  Gracia in Barcelona
partly because in your orange shirt you look like a
  better happier St. Sebastian
partly because of my love for you, partly because of
  your love for yoghurt
partly because of the fluorescent orange tulips around
  the birches
partly because of the secrecy our smiles take on before
  people and statuary
it is hard to believe when I'm with you that there can
  be anything as still
as solemn as unpleasantly definitive as statuary when
  right in front of it
in the warm New York 4 o'clock light we are drifting
  back and forth
between each other like a tree breathing through its
  spectacles

and the portrait show seems to have no faces in it at
    all, just paint
you suddenly wonder why in the world anyone ever
    did them
                                          I look
at you and I would rather look at you than all the
    portraits in the world
except possibly for the *Polish Rider* occasionally and
    anyway it's in the Frick
which thank heavens you haven't gone to yet so we can
    go together the first time
and the fact that you move so beautifully more or less
    takes care of Futurism
just as at home I never think of the *Nude Descending a*
    Staircase or
at a rehearsal a single drawing of Leonardo or
    Michelangelo that used to wow me
and what good does all the research of the
    Impressionists do them
when they never got the right person to stand near the
    tree when the sun sank

or for that matter Marino Marini when he didn't pick
   the rider as carefully
as the horse
           it seems they were all cheated of some
              marvellous experience
which is not going to go wasted on me which is why
   I'm telling you about it

Frank O'Hara

Ironing

I used to iron everything:
my iron flying over sheets and towels
like a sledge chased by wolves over snow,

the flex twisting and crinking
until the sheath frayed, exposing
wires like nerves. I stood like a horse

with a smoking hoof
inviting anyone who dared
to lie on my silver-padded board,

to be pressed to the thinness
of dolls cut from paper.
I'd have commandeered a crane

if I could, got the welders at Jarrow
to heat me an iron the size of a tug
to flatten the house.

Then for years I ironed nothing.
I put the iron in a high cupboard.
I converted to crumpledness.

And now I iron again: shaking
dark spots of water onto wrinkled
silk, nosing into sleeves, round

buttons, breathing the sweet heated smell
hot metal draws from newly-washed
cloth, until my blouse dries

to a shining, creaseless blue,
an airy shape with room to push
my arms, breasts, lungs, heart into.

Vicki Feaver

'Repeat that, repeat'

Repeat that, repeat,
Cuckoo, bird, and open ear wells, heart-springs,
    delightfully sweet,
With a ballad, with a ballad, a rebound
Off trundled timber and scoops of the hillside ground,
    hollow hollow hollow ground:
The whole landscape flushes on a sudden at a sound.

Gerard Manley Hopkins

On Roofs of Terry Street

Television aerials, Chinese characters
In the lower sky, wave gently in the smoke.

Nest-building sparrows peck at moss,
Urban flora and fauna, soft, unscrupulous.

Rain drying on the slates shines sometimes.
A builder is repairing someone's leaking roof,

He kneels upright to rest his back,
His trowel catches the light and becomes precious.

Douglas Dunn

The Deep Heart's Core

The Deep Heart's Core

A popular treatment for anxiety makes use of a practice called creative visualisation, in which the patient engages all their senses to imagine in detail a place where they can feel calm and safe. Studies involving war veterans suffering from post-traumatic stress disorder have shown the technique to be hugely beneficial. In fact, this kind of mind-travel is something we all do automatically. As a species, we are unusually adept at daydreaming – witness the many accounts of prisoners and hostages who imagine themselves away from the horror of their surroundings.

Yeats believed that imagined worlds of this kind are located 'in the deep heart's core', and as such can be visited at any time, so that it's possible at the same moment to be in the midst of the rush and clamour of life and a million miles away from it. Yeats's own experience bears this out. While walking down a busy Fleet Street, he found himself pausing to look at a fountain in a shop window display. The sound of trickling water transported him back at once to the setting of his childhood summers; a small, uninhabited island where the tranquil evenings were 'full of the linnet's wings'.

Not all the imagined worlds you'll find in these pages offer solace, though each one may be called a sanctum. They are sacred places, places of solitude, places where the soul has room to expand and stillness enough to hear itself think. When Robert Frost stops to watch a stranger's woods 'fill up with snow' we understand that what he has stumbled on is the hushed province of death itself. A shake of harness bells from his waiting horse reminds the speaker that there is still far too much to be done to enter the woods right now; he continues on his way.

In Alice Oswald's 'Aside', a laurel bush beside a house remembered from childhood becomes a 'Museum of Twilight' into which she pushes her way and remains while 'by degrees I became invisible'. The Norwegian poet Olav H. Hauge describes how he piles up his words into a poem to make 'something like a house'. His enterprise reminds us that all poems contain rooms to be visited ('stanza' is Italian for 'a room') but Hauge's express purpose is to recapture the magic of the leaf-huts and snow-houses he built in days when he was small enough 'to creep in and sit / listening to the rain'.

Derek Mahon conjures a different kind of sanctum altogether: a shelter for all our unlived futures, where each abandoned possibility is represented by a dead leaf. The image has something in common with what quantum physicists refer to as the 'many worlds interpretation', in which the past is pictured as a thickly-branched tree, signifying all the choices we've encountered at various junctures in our lives. Those choices, say the physicists, aren't lost: they exist alongside us, as parallel worlds. But Mahon's vision is more subtle than that: his 'stadium' becomes a beguiling storehouse of what might have been, a hushed and holy space 'filled with an infinite / Rustling and sighing'.

These are poems to wander about in and commit to memory so they can be stored away in the deep heart's core; places of solitude to find and lose yourself in; places to visit and return to at will.

Aside

In Berkshire somewhere 1970
I hid in a laurel bush outside a house,
planted in gravel I think.
I stopped running and just pushed open
its oilskin flaps and settled down
in some kind of waiting room, whose scarred boughs
had clearly been leaning and kneeling there
for a long time. They were bright black.

I remember this Museum of Twilight
was low-ceilinged and hear-through
as through a bedroom window
one hears the zone of someone's afternoon
being shouted and shouted in, but by now
I was too evergreen to answer, watching
the woodlice at work in hard hats
taking their trolleys up and down.

through longer and longer interims
a dead leaf fell, rigidly yellow and slow,
so by degrees I became invisible

in that spotted sick-room light
and nobody found me there,
the hour has not yet ended in which
under a cloth of laurel
I sat quite still.

Alice Oswald

Leaf-Huts and Snow-Houses

There's not much to
these verses, only
a few words piled up
at random.
I think
nonetheless
it's fine
to make them, then
for a little while
I have something like a house.
I remember leaf-huts
we built
when we were small:
to creep in and sit
listening to the rain,
feel alone in the wilderness,
drops on your nose
and your hair –
Or snow-houses at Christmas,
to creep in and
close the hole with a sack,

light a candle and stay there
on cold evenings.

Olav H. Hauge
tr. Robin Fulton

Stopping by Woods on a Snowy Evening

Whose woods these are I think I know.
His house is in the village, though;
He will not see me stopping here
To watch his woods fill up with snow.

My little horse must think it queer
To stop without a farmhouse near
Between the woods and frozen lake
The darkest evening of the year.

He gives his harness bells a shake
To ask if there is some mistake.
The only other sound's the sweep
Of easy wind and downy flake.

The woods are lovely, dark, and deep.
But I have promises to keep,
And miles to go before I sleep,
And miles to go before I sleep.

Robert Frost

Lights Out

I have come to the borders of sleep,
The unfathomable deep
Forest where all must lose
Their way, however straight,
Or winding, soon or late;
They cannot choose.

Many a road and track
That, since the dawn's first crack,
Up to the forest brink,
Deceived the travellers
Suddenly now blurs,
And in they sink.

Here love ends,
Despair, ambition ends,
All pleasure and all trouble,
Although most sweet or bitter,
Here ends in sleep that is sweeter
Than tasks most noble.

There is not any book
Or face of dearest look
That I would not turn from now
To go into the unknown
I must enter and leave alone
I know not how.

The tall forest towers;
Its cloudy foliage lowers
Ahead, shelf above shelf;
Its silence I hear and obey
That I may lose my way
And myself.

Edward Thomas

Daystar

She wanted a little room for thinking:
but she saw diapers steaming on the line,
a doll slumped behind the door.

So she lugged a chair behind the garage
to sit out the children's naps.

Sometimes there were things to watch –
the pinched armor of a vanished cricket,
a floating maple leaf. Other days
she stared until she was assured
when she closed her eyes
she'd see only her own vivid blood.

She had an hour, at best, before Liza appeared
pouting from the top of the stairs.
And just *what* was mother doing
out back with the field mice? Why,
building a palace. Later
that night when Thomas rolled over and
lurched into her, she would open her eyes

and think of the place that was hers
for an hour – where
she was nothing,
pure nothing, in the middle of the day.

Rita Dove

The Fields of Dark

The wreathing vine within the porch
Is in the heart of me,
The roses that the noondays scorch
Shall burn in memory;
Alone at night I quench the light,
And without star or spark
The grass and trees press to my knees,
And flowers throng the dark.

The leaves that loose their hold at noon
Drop on my face like rain,
And in the watches of the moon
I feel them fall again.
By day I stray how far away
To stream and wood and steep,
But on my track they all come back
To haunt the vale of sleep.

The fields of light are clover-brimmed,
Or grassed or daisy-starred,
The fields of dark are softly dimmed,

And safely twi-light barred;
But in the gloom that fills my room
I cannot fail to mark
The grass and trees about my knees,
The flowers in the dark.

Ethelwyn Wetherald

Heaven-Haven

A nun takes the veil

I have desired to go
    Where springs not fail,
To fields where flies no sharp and sided hail
    And a few lilies blow.

And I have asked to be
    Where no storms come,
Where the green swell is in the havens dumb,
    And out of the swing of the sea.

Gerard Manley Hopkins

The Room

'When I die I will return to seek
The moments I did not live by the sea'
—Sophia de Mello Breyner

It has always been waiting,
long windows down to the dusty floorboards,
golden brown tea as good as I drank
out of pink and white cups
in the Convent of Mercy thirty years ago.
John McCormack on the record player,
hot cross buns and butter,
the ocean below rising in grey sheets
same colour as my coat
which hangs by the door.
In a moment, I put it on,
walk on the sand
with the spray on my face.

Martina Evans

Canopy

The weather was inside.

The branches trembled over the glass as if to apologise; then they thumped and they came in.

And the trees shook everything off until they were bare and clean. They held on to the ground with their long feet and leant into the gale and back again.

This was their way with the wind.

They flung us down and flailed above us with their visions and their pale tree light.

I think they were telling us to survive. That's what a leaf feels like anyway. We lay under their great awry display and they tattooed us with light.

They got inside us and made us speak; I said my first word in their language: canopy'.

I was crying and it felt like I was feeding. Be my
mother, I said to the trees, in the language of trees,
which can't be transcribed, and they shook their hair
back, and they bent low with their many arms, and
they looked into my eyes as only trees can look into
the eyes of a person, they touched me with the rain on
their fingers till I was all droplets, till I was a mist, and
they said they would.

Emily Berry

Floating Island

Harmonious powers with nature work
On sky, earth, river, lake and sea
Sunshine and cloud, whirlwind and breeze,
All in one duteous task agree.

Once did I see a slip of earth
By throbbing waves long undermined,
Loosed from its hold – how, no one knew,
But all might see it float, obedient to the wind,

Might see it from the mossy shore
Dissevered, float upon the lake,
Float with its crest of trees adorned
On which the warbling birds their pastime take.

Food, shelter, safety, there they find;
There berries ripen, flowerets bloom;
There insects live their lives – and die:
A peopled world it is, in size a tiny room.

And thus through many seasons' space
This little island may survive,
But nature (though we mark her not)
Will take away, may cease to give.

Perchance when you are wandering forth
Upon some vacant sunny day
Without an object, hope, or fear,
Thither your eyes may turn – the isle is passed away,

Buried beneath the glittering lake,
Its place no longer to be found.
Yet the lost fragments shall remain
To fertilize some other ground.

Dorothy Wordsworth

Lighthouse

My son's awake at ten, stretched out along
his bunk beneath the ceiling, wired and watchful.
The end of August. Already the high-flung
daylight sky of our Northern solstice dulls
earlier and earlier to a clouded bowl;
his Star of David lamp and plastic moon
have turned the dusk to dark outside his room.

Across the Lough, where ferries venture blithely
and once a cruise ship, massive as a palace,
inched its brilliant decks to open sea—
a lighthouse starts its own nightlong address
in fractured signalling; it blinks and bats
the swingball of its beam, then stands to catch,
then hurls it out again beyond its parallax.

He counts each creamy loop inside his head,
each well-black interval, and thinks it just for him—
this gesture from a world that can't be entered:
the two of them partly curtained, partly seen,

upheld in a sort of boy-talk conversation
no one else can hear. That private place, it answers,
with birds and slatted windows—I've been there.

Sinead Morrissey

The Lake Isle of Innisfree

I will arise and go now, and go to Innisfree,
And a small cabin build there, of clay and wattles made:
Nine bean-rows will I have there, a hive for the
   honey-bee,
And live alone in the bee-loud glade.

And I shall have some peace there, for peace
   comes dropping slow,
Dropping from the veils of the morning to where
   the cricket sings;
There midnight's all a glimmer, and noon a purple
   glow,
And evening full of the linnet's wings.

I will arise and go now, for always night and day
I hear lake water lapping with low sounds by the shore;
While I stand on the roadway, or on the pavements
   grey,
I hear it in the deep heart's core.

W. B. Yeats

Leaves

The prisoners of infinite choice
Have built their house
In a field below the wood
And are at peace.

It is autumn, and dead leaves
On their way to the river
Scratch like birds at the windows
Or tick on the road.

Somewhere there is an afterlife
Of dead leaves,
A stadium filled with an infinite
Rustling and sighing.

Somewhere in the heaven
Of lost futures
The lives we might have lived
Have found their own fulfilment.

Derek Mahon

Look We Have Coming to Dover!

'*So various, so beautiful, so new...*'
—Matthew Arnold, 'Dover Beach'

Stowed in the sea to invade
the alfresco lash of a diesel-breeze
ratcheting speed into the tide, brunt with
gobfuls of surf phlegmed by cushy come-and-go
tourists prow'd on the cruisers, lording the ministered
    waves.

Seagull and shoal life
vexing their blarnies upon our huddled
camouflage past the vast crumble of scummed
cliffs, scramming on mulch as thunder unbladders
yobbish rain and wind on our escape hutched in a
    Bedford van.

Seasons or years we reap
inland, unclocked by the national eye
or stabs in the back, teemed for breathing

sweeps of grass through the whistling asthma of parks,
burdened, ennobled – poling sparks across pylon and
   pylon.

Swarms of us, grafting in
the black within shot of the moon's
spotlight, banking on the miracle of sun –
span its rainbow, passport us to life. Only then
can it be human to hoick ourselves, bare-faced for the
   clear.

Imagine my love and I,
our sundry others, Blair'd in the cash
of our beeswax'd cars, our crash clothes, free,
we raise our charged glasses over unparasol'd tables
East, babbling our lingoes, flecked by the chalk of
   Britannia!

   Daljit Nagra

Sea-Fever

I must go down to the seas again, to the lonely sea and
the sky,
And all I ask is a tall ship and a star to steer her by,
And the wheel's kick and the wind's song and the white
sails shaking,
And a grey mist on the sea's face and a grey dawn
breaking.

I must go down to the seas again, for the call of the
running tide
Is a wild call and a clear call that may not be denied;
And all I ask is a windy day with the white clouds flying,
And the flung spray and the blown spume, and the
sea-gulls crying.

I must go down to the seas again, to the vagrant gypsy
life,
To the gull's way and the whale's way where the wind's
like a whetted knife;
And all I ask is a merry yarn from a laughing
fellow-rover,

And quiet sleep and a sweet dream when the long
trick's over.

John Masefield

Birches

When I see birches bend to left and right
Across the lines of straighter darker trees,
I like to think some boy's been swinging them.
But swinging doesn't bend them down to stay
As ice storms do. Often you must have seen them
Loaded with ice a sunny winter morning
After a rain. They click upon themselves
As the breeze rises, and turn many-colored
As the stir cracks and crazes their enamel.
Soon the sun's warmth makes them shed crystal shells
Shattering and avalanching on the snow crust –
Such heaps of broken glass to sweep away
You'd think the inner dome of heaven had fallen.
They are dragged to the withered bracken by the load,
And they seem not to break; though once they are
    bowed
So low for long, they never right themselves:
You may see their trunks arching in the woods
Years afterwards, trailing their leaves on the ground
Like girls on hands and knees that throw their hair
Before them over their heads to dry in the sun.

But I was going to say when Truth broke in
With all her matter of fact about the ice storm,
I should prefer to have some boy bend them
As he went out and in to fetch the cows –
Some boy too far from town to learn baseball,
Whose only play was what he found himself,
Summer or winter, and could play alone.
One by one he subdued his father's trees
By riding them down over and over again
Until he took the stiffness out of them,
And not one but hung limp, not one was left
For him to conquer. He learned all there was
To learn about not launching out too soon
And so not carrying the tree away
Clear to the ground. He always kept his poise
To the top branches, climbing carefully
With the same pains you use to fill a cup
Up to the brim, and even above the brim.
Then he flung outward, feet first, with a swish,
Kicking his way down through the air to the ground.
So was I once myself a swinger of birches.

And so I dream of going back to be.
It's when I'm weary of considerations,
And life is too much like a pathless wood
Where your face burns and tickles with the cobwebs
Broken across it, and one eye is weeping
From a twig's having lashed across it open.
I'd like to get away from earth awhile
And then come back to it and begin over.
May no fate willfully misunderstand me
And half grant what I wish and snatch me away
Not to return. Earth's the right place for love:
I don't know where it's likely to go better.
I'd like to go by climbing a birch tree,
And climb black branches up a snow-white trunk
Toward heaven, till the tree could bear no more,
But dipped its top and set me down again.
That would be good both going and coming back.
One could do worse than be a swinger of birches.

Robert Frost

The Boat

i.m. Seamus Heaney

Take the case of a man in a boat
in deep water. The wind and the waves
and the craft's tossing cause him to stumble
if he makes to stand up, for, no matter how firmly
he tries to hold on, through the boat's slithering
he bends and he staggers, so unstable
the body is. And yet he is safe.

It's the same with the righteous:
if they fall, they are falling only
like a man in a boat who is safe and sound
as long as he stays within the boat's timbers.

Piers Plowman, passus 8

Bernard O'Donoghue

Arracombe Wood

Some said, because he wud'n spaik
    Any words to women but Yes and No,
Nor put out his hand for Parson to shake
    He mun be bird-witted. But I do go
    By the lie of the barley that he did sow,
And I wish no better thing than to hold a rake
    Like Dave, in his time, or to see him mow.

    Put up in churchyard a month ago,
'A bitter old soul,' they said, but it wadn't so.
His heart were in Arracombe Wood where he'd used
    to go
To sit and talk wi' his shadder till sun went low,
Though what it was all about us'll never know.
    And there baint no mem'ry in the place
    Of th' old man's footmark, nor his face;
    Arracombe Wood do think more of a crow –
'Will be violets there in the Spring: in Summer time
    the spider's lace;
    And come the Fall, the whizzle and race

Of the dry, dead leaves when the wind gies chase;
And on the Eve of Christmas, fallin' snow.

Charlotte Mew

A Blessing

Just off the highway to Rochester, Minnesota,
Twilight bounds softly forth on the grass.
And the eyes of those two Indian ponies
Darken with kindness.
They have come gladly out of the willows
To welcome my friend and me.
We step over the barbed wire into the pasture
Where they have been grazing all day, alone.
They ripple tensely, they can hardly contain their
    happiness
That we have come.
They bow shyly as wet swans. They love each other.
There is no loneliness like theirs.
At home once more,
They begin munching the young tufts of spring in the
    darkness.
I would like to hold the slenderer one in my arms,
For she has walked over to me
And nuzzled my left hand.
She is black and white,
Her mane falls wild on her forehead,

And the light breeze moves me to caress her long ear
That is delicate as the skin over a girl's wrist.
Suddenly I realize
That if I stepped out of my body I would break
Into blossom.

James Wright

To Sleep

O soft embalmer of the still midnight,
    Shutting, with careful fingers and benign,
Our gloom-pleas'd eyes, embower'd from the light,
    Enshaded in forgetfulness divine:
O soothest Sleep! if so it please thee, close
    In midst of this thine hymn my willing eyes,
Or wait the "Amen," ere thy poppy throws
    Around my bed its lulling charities.
Then save me, or the passed day will shine
Upon my pillow, breeding many woes,—
    Save me from curious Conscience, that still lords
Its strength for darkness, burrowing like a mole;
    Turn the key deftly in the oiled wards,
And seal the hushed Casket of my Soul.

John Keats

The scent of apple cake

My mother cooked as drudgery
the same fifteen dishes round
and round like a donkey bound
to a millstone grinding dust.

My mother baked as a dance,
the flour falling from the sifter
in a rain of fine white pollen.
The sugar was sweet snow.

The dough beneath her palms
was the warm flesh of a baby
when they were all hers before
their wills sprouted like mushrooms.

Cookies she formed in rows
on the baking sheets, oatmeal,
molasses, lemon, chocolate chip,
delights anyone could love.

Love was in short supply,
but pies were obedient to her
command of their pastry, crisp
holding the sweetness within.

Desserts were her reward for endless
cleaning in the acid yellow cloud
of Detroit, begging dollars from
my father, mending, darning, bleaching.

In the oven she made sweetness
where otherwise there was none.

Marge Piercy

The Red Sea

for Margaret

When we go to the house together for the last time,
they've taken the floor-coverings up in the kitchen.
I see what was always there but had forgotten:
red cement, with a green diamond at the centre –
where we've been placed with dolls and animals
in the upturned softwood bench, so scored and scribbled
with woodworm you say it's our secret script.
There's a taint in the air of white spirit. Our mother
is on her knees, working towards the open door.
Later she'll reach a plank across the wet paint
and rescue us. But for now the bench is our boat.
I'm gripping a hurley and rowing us in her pursuit.

Maurice Riordan

Visible, Invisible

Visible, Invisible

The title of this final section is taken from Marianne Moore's eight-line poem 'A Jellyfish', about a creature that enthrals but – in spite of the speaker's best efforts – remains resolutely out of reach. But while the physical creature defies capture by hand, Moore succeeds instead in capturing its pulsating expansion and contraction by her use of alternating four- and three-beat lines, and in showing us the 'amber-tinctured amethyst' that inhabits the animal. Like all the poems gathered here, this jewel-like lyric reminds us that there are rewards to be had from stepping out of the bustle of our own activity in order simply to be and observe.

From time to time, circumstances force us to do just that. In Dante Gabriel Rossetti's 'The Woodspurge', it is grief that causes the speaker's world to slow and narrow to such an extent that he notices the tiny, three-headed flower blossoming near his feet. Denise Riley, similarly stopped in her tracks (this time by illness), notes precisely how the branches move on a tree seen from her sickbed – how 'One branch catches a notion of movement, / shivering, then the rest cotton on in a rush'. Centuries apart, these two poets share an insight: among the busy dailiness of life, it's easy for the things of the world to pass us by; in the midst of despair, a new way of looking is stumbled on.

Many of the poems you'll find here are about looking closely enough and in such a way that the invisible is made visible once more. Observing with that level of intensity isn't easy (the speaker of Matthew Francis's 'Ant' eventually resorts to dunking his subject in brandy in order to get a good look at it) but these poems show us that it is always worthwhile. Often, the harder we look the less familiar the object of our gaze turns out to be: a fork becomes the clawed foot of some prehistoric bird; lichen is like a horde of black and golden ears; houseflies have wings like flakes of dead skin; and a young woman in a wheelchair turns her wheels with the energy and expert timing of a concert pianist restating a fading chord.

In his famous poem 'Leisure', W. H. Davies poses the question 'What is life if, full of care, / we have no time to stand and stare.' In a world in which our senses are frequently overloaded to the point of numbness, the defamiliarisation that comes from such staring provides a powerful remedy. With practice, it can return the world to us anew.

A Spider

I trapped a spider in a glass,
a fine-blown wineglass.
It shut around him, silently.
He stood still, a small wheel
of intricate suspension, cap
at the hub of his eight spokes,
inked eyes on stalks; alert,
sensing a difference.
I meant to let him go
but still he taps against the glass
all Marcel Marceau
in *the wall that is there but not there*,
a circumstance I know.

Colette Bryce

Tree seen from bed

The fuller leaves are ridged, the newer red.
Sunshine is pooled over them, like lacquer.
One branch catches a notion of movement,
shivering, then the rest cotton on in a rush
roused by the wind, to thrash and vacillate.
A toss-up, where they'll all go next – to lash
around through summer until autumn, that
is where; to fall. May it be managed lightly
though it could well turn wilder beforehand.
Tree watched from my sickbed, read to me.
Read from the hymnal of frank life – of how
to be old, yet never rehearse that fact cosily.

Denise Riley

The Woodspurge

The wind flapped loose, the wind was still,
Shaken out dead from tree and hill:
I had walked on at the wind's will, –
I sat now, for the wind was still.

Between my knees my forehead was, –
My lips, drawn in, said not Alas!
My hair was over in the grass,
My naked ears heard the day pass.

My eyes, wide open, had the run
Of some ten weeds to fix upon;
Among those few, out of the sun,
The woodspurge flowered, three cups in one.

From perfect grief there need not be
Wisdom or even memory:
One thing then learnt remains to me, –
The woodspurge has a cup of three.

Dante Gabriel Rossetti

Flies

This is the day the flies fall awake mid-sentence
and lie stunned on the window-sill shaking with
   speeches
only it isn't speech it is trembling sections of
   puzzlement which
break off suddenly as if the questioner had been shot

this is one of those wordy days
when they drop from their winter quarters in the
   curtains and sizzle as they fall
feeling like old cigarette butts called back to life
blown from the surface of some charred world

and somehow their wings which are little more than
   flakes of dead skin
have carried them to this blackened disembodied
   question

what dirt shall we visit today?
what dirt shall we re-visit?

they lift their faces to the past and walk about a bit
trying out their broken thought-machines
coming back with their used-up words

there is such a horrible trapped buzzing wherever we fly
it's going to be impossible to think clearly now until
     next winter
what should we
what dirt should we

   Alice Oswald

Fork

This strange thing must have crept
Right out of hell.
It resembles a bird's foot
Worn around the cannibal's neck.

As you hold it in your hand,
As you stab with it into a piece of meat,
It is possible to imagine the rest of the bird:
Its head which like your fist
Is large, bald, beakless and blind.

Charles Simic

Cabbage

I ask the garden to bear me witness
but what the ground offers me as evening comes
looks most of all like a snoozing face –
whorled, shut, deaf to disgrace –
a mute Om from a drill of Oms,
cool leaves creaking – a Northern lotus.

Jen Hadfield

Cats Are Otherwise

Cat steps into the house; courteous,
But still privately electrified by the garden. His fur,
Plump with light as the breastfeathers of the young
    god of air,
Implies brush-bruised geraniums, and herbs:
Fruitmusk webs of blackcurrant groves
Rusting slowly in an old sun:
A slow-unrolling afternoon
Asleep on the warm earth, above fresh bird-bones.

Cats know control as the basis of magic.
They are our slimmer selves,
That peel doors open to slip out – all eyes – and are
    gone;
May or may not report back
The easy cruelties of the perfectly adapted, the
    over-civilized.

When they yawn, a hot zigzag rose blown deep open
Amazes with its pinkness.
The yawn seems bigger than their whole head, like a
     snake's.
Two eyes slip, soft yolks on a bone brink, right back
     into their ears.

Cats may not care to offer up each thought. We look
     on them;
And remain, like children on the stairs at a dinner party,
Acknowledged by that other world,
Yet uninvited; and so not fully present.

Katherine Pierpoint

'Adieu foulard...'

(Chapter X from 'Tales of the Islands')

I watched the island narrowing the fine
Writing of foam around the precipices, then
The roads as small and casual as twine
Thrown on its mountains; I watched till the plane
Turned to the final north and turned above
The open channel with the grey sea between
The fishermen's islets until all that I love
Folded in cloud; I watched the shallow green
That broke in places where there would be reef,
The silver glinting on the fuselage, each mile
Dividing us and all fidelity strained
Till space would snap it. Then, after a while
I thought of nothing; nothing, I prayed,
    would change;
When we set down at Seawell it had rained.

Derek Walcott

A Phone off the Hook

Left for five minutes
it starts up a wail, a siren,
its own private emergency.

It's the agony
of being left like this, open
but with the connection broken.

It would rather have whatever
you might spit or whisper into it
than this. The receiver put down wrong,

balanced at a bad angle
like a broken bone,
and no one coming to mend it.

Jean Sprackland

Goldfinches

In the fields
we let them have –
in the fields
we don't want yet –

where thistles rise
out of the marshlands of spring, and spring open –
each bud
a settlement of riches –

a coin of reddish fire –
the finches
wait for midsummer,
for the long days,

for the brass heat,
for the seeds to begin to form in the hardening thistles,
dazzling as the teeth of mice,
but black,

filling the face of every flower.
Then they drop from the sky.
A buttery gold,
they swing on the thistles, they gather

the silvery down, they carry it
in their finchy beaks
to the edges of the fields,
to the trees,

as though their minds were on fire
with the flower of one perfect idea –
and there they build their nests
and lay their pale-blue eggs,

every year,
and every year
the hatchlings wake in the swaying branches,
in the silver baskets,

and love the world.
Is it necessary to say any more?
Have you heard them singing in the wind, above the
final fields?
Have you ever been so happy in your life?

Mary Oliver

A Rainy Morning

A young woman in a wheelchair,
wearing a black nylon poncho spattered with rain,
is pushing herself through the morning.
You have seen how pianists
sometimes bend forward to strike the keys,
then lift their hands, draw back to rest,
then lean again to strike just as the chord fades.
Such is the way this woman
strikes at the wheels, then lifts her long white fingers,
letting them float, then bends again to strike
just as the chair slows, as if into a silence.
So expertly she plays the chords
of this difficult music she has mastered,
her wet face beautiful in its concentration,
while the wind turns the pages of rain.

Ted Kooser

Mushrooms

Overnight, very
Whitely, discreetly,
Very quietly

Our toes, our noses
Take hold on the loam,
Acquire the air.

Nobody sees us,
Stops us, betrays us;
The small grains make room.

Soft fists insist on
Heaving the needles,
The leafy bedding,

Even the paving.
Our hammers, our rams,
Earless and eyeless,

Perfectly voiceless,
Widen the crannies,

Shoulder through holes. We

Diet on water,
On crumbs of shadow,
Bland-mannered, asking

Little or nothing.
So many of us!
So many of us!

We are shelves, we are
Tables, we are meek,
We are edible,

Nudgers and shovers
In spite of ourselves.
Our kind multiplies:

We shall by morning
Inherit the earth.
Our foot's in the door.

Sylvia Plath

Laying the Dust

What a sweet smell rises
     when you lay the dust –
bucket after bucket of water thrown
on the yellow grass.
                    The water
flashes
each time you
make it leap –
          arching its glittering back.
The sound of
               more water
pouring into the pail
almost quenches my thirst.
Surely when flowers
grow here, they'll not
smell sweeter than this
               wet ground, suddenly black.

Denise Levertov

Ant

after Robert Hooke, *Micrographia*

All afternoon a reddish trickle
    out of the roots of the beech
      and across the lawn,
a sort of rust that shines and dances.
    Close up, it proves to be ant,
      each droplet a horned
traveller finicking its way round
    the crooked geometry
      of a grass forest.
A finger felled in their path rocks them,
    amazed, back on their haunches.
      I see them tasting
the air for subtle intelligence,
    till one ventures to scale it,
      and others follow.

They are fidgety subjects to draw.
    If you sink the feet in glue
      the rest twists and writhes;
kill one, the juices evaporate
    in seconds, leaving only

the shrivelled casing.
I dunked one in brandy. It struggled
    till the air rose from its mouth
        in pinprick bubbles.
I let it soak an hour, then dried it,
    observed the spherical head,
        the hairlike feelers,
the grinning vice of its sideways jaw,
    the coppery armour plate
        with its scattered spines.

Some draught stirred it then. It rose to all
    its feet, and set off across
        the rough miles of desk.

Matthew Francis

The Windhover

To Christ our Lord

I caught this morning morning's minion, king-
  dom of daylight's dauphin, dapple-dawn-drawn
    Falcon, in his riding
  Of the rolling level underneath him steady air, and
    striding
High there, how he rung upon the rein of a wimpling
  wing
In his ecstasy! then off, off forth on swing,
  As a skate's heel sweeps smooth on a bow-bend: the
    hurl and gliding
  Rebuffed the big wind. My heart in hiding
Stirred for a bird,—the achieve of, the mastery of the
  thing!

Brute beauty and valour and act, oh, air, pride, plume,
  here
  Buckle! AND the fire that breaks from thee then, a
    billion
Times told lovelier, more dangerous, O my chevalier!

No wonder of it: shéer plód makes plough down
    sillion
Shine, and blue-bleak embers, ah my dear,
    Fall, gall themselves, and gash gold-vermilion.

Gerard Manley Hopkins

Lichen

Who listens
like lichen listens

assiduous millions of black
and golden ears?

You hear

        and remember

but I'm speaking
to the lichen.

The little ears prunk,
scorch and blacken.

The little golden
mouths gape

    Jen Hadfield

Walrus

His grotesque tusks are half
Broken off,
Result of a long-lost territorial
Tussle. A little brilliantine
Would surely work wonders
On his bristles,
The disorderly stubble

That sprouts around his mouth. Dozy
Old relic, earless
Wonder, his phenomenal wealth of blubber
Comes from a lifetime's sucking up
Of delectable molluscs, raw; neither
Of his flippers is enough
To keep him upright underwater

Now. Tremulously
His whiskers twitch, sift the dirt
On the ocean floor, feel for more
Shells to slurp meat from. He won't last
Another year

In the colony. Poor pinniped
Without a harem to rule, fat bastard

Upholstered in barnacled skin, he levers
Himself out of the sea by his tusks; the others
Ignore him. He cuddles up
To a convenient
Rock, his immobile bulk an obstacle course
Of wrinkles. Soon the ice pack
Will break up

And strand him. It's almost comical
How unaware of the future he seems –
As if the answer
Ties under the black Atlantic
Waters around him. The waves
Bob glossily off
In the distance, the clams keep breathing
Quietly through their shells. They open
And close like hands, waiting
To measure out their applause.

Jane Yeh

A Jellyfish

Visible, invisible,
   a fluctuating charm
an amber-tinctured amethyst
   inhabits it, your arm
approaches and it opens
   and it closes; you had meant
to catch it and it quivers;
   you abandon your intent.

Marianne Moore

Notes

1. 'Oscillations of heart rate and respiration synchronize during poetry recitation': Dirk Cysarz, Dietrich von Bonin, Helmut Lackner, Peter Heusser, Maximilian Moser and Henrik Bettermann. First published in *American Journal of Physiology – Heart and Circulatory Physiology*, Vol. 287, Issue 2 (Aug 2004), pp. 579–587.
2. 'The Neural Lyre: Poetic Meter, the Brain, and Time' by Ernst Pöppel and Frederick Turner. First published in *Poetry* magazine, Vol. 142, No. 5 (Aug. 1983), pp. 277–309. The authors won the Levinson Prize for this groundbreaking essay.

Author Biographies

Fleur Adcock (1934–) was born in Auckland, New Zealand, but spent much of her childhood in England, returning to live in London in 1963. She is known for her poised, witty, lyric poems, which explore themes of identity, gender and rootlessness. She is the author of ten books of poetry, and a collected works, *Poems 1960–2000*, was published in 2000. She was awarded an OBE in 1996.

Simon Armitage (1963–) was born in Huddersfield and his work is characterised by its dry, Yorkshire wit and deadpan tone. He is the author of numerous collections of poetry including *The Dead Sea Poems* (1995), *Killing Time* (1999), *Universal Home Doctor* (2002), *The Shout: Selected Poems* (2005), *The Not Dead* (2008) and *Seeing Stars* (2010). In 2015 he was elected Oxford Professor of Poetry.

Fiona Benson (1978–) won an Eric Gregory Award in 2006 and a Faber New Poets Award in 2009. Her first collection, *Bright Travellers*, was nominated for the T. S. Eliot Prize and won the 2015 Seamus Heaney Centre Prize for a First Full Collection and the 2015 Geoffrey Faber Memorial Prize. Her second collection is the acclaimed *Vertigo & Ghost* (2019).

Emily Berry (1981–) is the author of *Dear Boy* (2013), which won the Hawthornden Prize and the Forward Prize for Best First Collection, and *Stranger Baby* (2017), both published by Faber & Faber. She is the editor of *The Poetry Review*, the UK's most widely read poetry magazine. She was selected as a Next Generation poet by the Poetry Book Society in 2014.

Robert Bly (1926–) was born in Madison, Minnesota, and is the author of more than thirty books of poetry. His first collection, *Silence in the Snowy Fields* (1962) was extremely influential for the simplicity of its language and imagery rooted in the natural world. Bly's literary magazine for poetry in translation (*The Fifties, Sixties* and *Seventies*) published the work of many previously unknown European and South American poets, introducing them to an American audience for the first time.

Robert Browning (1812–1889) is now regarded as one of the most important poets of the Victorian period, though his poetry was often misjudged by his contemporaries. He married the poet Elizabeth Barrett in 1846 and they lived in Italy until her death in 1862. Browning then returned to London and the publication of his long narrative poem, *The Ring and the Book*, finally brought him success and recognition. He is buried in Poets' Corner in Westminster Abbey.

Colette Bryce (1970–) was born in Derry, Northern Ireland. She has published four poetry collections including *The Full Indian Rope Trick* (2004) and *Self-Portrait in the Dark* (2008). She received the Cholmondeley Award for poetry in 2010 and her *Selected Poems* won the Pigott Prize for Irish Poetry 2017. She was Editor of *Poetry London* from 2009 to 2013.

Charles Causley (1917–2003) was born in Launceston, Cornwall, where he spent most of his life. His poetry is rooted in the Cornish landscape and its myths and legends. His writing fell outside the poetic trends of his time and he was a master of traditional forms. Ted Hughes described him as one of the 'best loved and most needed' poets of his generation.

Margaret Cavendish, Duchess of Newcastle-upon-Tyne (1623–1673), was born in Colchester in Essex, but as a young woman became Maid of Honour to the exiled Queen Henrietta Maria. In spite of a limited education and a natural reticence, Margaret was one of the most prolific and controversial female writers of her time. Her first book, *Poems and Fancies* (from which her poem 'Of Many Worlds in this World' is taken), was published in 1653. Her writing on philosophy challenged the work of a number of leading thinkers of the day and was held in such regard that she became the first woman to be invited to attend a meeting at the Royal Society.

John Clare (1793–1864) was born into a peasant family in the village of Helpston, Northamptonshire, and was raised as an agricultural labourer. He is best known for his poetic celebrations of nature and rural life, often expressing his sadness at the changes the landscape was undergoing. Clare suffered from episodes of severe depression and in 1837 was committed to an asylum in Essex where he spent the rest of his life.

David Constantine (1944–) worked for thirty years as a lecturer in German at Durham and Oxford universities and was co-editor of *Modern Poetry in Translation* from 2004 to 2013. His collections include *Something for the Ghosts* (2002), which was shortlisted for the Whitbread Poetry Award; *Collected Poems* (2004), a Poetry Book Society Recommendation; and *Elder* (2014). His translation of Friedrich Hölderlin's *Selected Poems* won the European Poetry Translation Prize.

Robert Creeley (1926–2005) was one of the defining poets of the American counter-cultural scene, known primarily for his association with the experimental Black Mountain Poets. He published more than sixty books of poetry including *For Love: Poems 1950–60* (1960), in which he established his spare, minimalist style. He was admitted to the American Academy and Institute of Arts and Letters in 1988.

Iain Crichton-Smith (1928–1998) was born in Glasgow and grew up on the island of Lewis. He wrote in both English and Gaelic, and his writing was strongly influenced by Gaelic culture, history and landscapes. He was a highly prolific writer, publishing numerous collections of poetry, novels and short stories. He won multiple literary awards and was honoured with an OBE in 1980.

Elizabeth Daryush (1887–1977) was the daughter of British poet laureate Robert Bridges. Her poetry was traditional in style, and often critical of the upper-class society in which she lived. She married Ali Akbar Daryush and lived in Persia for four years, after which her poetry expressed a new awareness of social injustice. Though her work achieved little recognition during her lifetime, her *Selected Poems* and *Collected Poems* were published shortly before her death.

C. Day Lewis (1904–1972) was born in Ireland, the son of a clergyman. A friend and contemporary of W. H. Auden and Stephen Spender, he regarded himself as a voice of poetic and political revolution and was an active member of the Communist Party. As well as poetry he published literary criticism and, under the pseudonym Nicholas Blake, detective stories. He was poet laureate from 1968 until his death.

Emily Dickinson (1830–1886) was born in Amherst, Massachusetts, and lived an isolated, reclusive life. Along with Walt Whitman, she is considered the founder of a uniquely American poetic voice, with a brilliant and personal style and vision. Though prolific, she was not recognised during her lifetime and the first volume of her work was published posthumously in 1890.

John Donne (1572–1631) was best known for his witty and complex love poems and is considered the leading poet of the Metaphysical school. His sonnets, elegies and satires rely heavily on the use of inventive metaphorical conceit, and often explore abstract ideas. He is also noted for his religious verse, occasional poems, sermons and verse letters.

Keith Douglas (1920–1944) is regarded as one of the most important poets of the Second World War; he died aged twenty-four in the D-Day invasion of Normandy. His work stands out from the poetry of the best-known war poets for its avoidance of patriotism and protest in favour of detached reportage. His reputation was established posthumously by Ted Hughes's 1964 edition of his *Selected Poems*.

Rita Dove (1952–) was one of the top 100 high-school graduates in the US and a Presidential Scholar. She was a Fulbright Scholar in Germany and received her MFA from the Iowa Writers' Workshop. In 1993 she became the first African American, and the youngest person, to be appointed Poet Laureate Consultant by the Library of Congress. Her collection *Thomas and Beulah* was awarded the 1987 Pulitzer Prize.

Carol Ann Duffy (1955–) was appointed Poet Laureate in 2009, the first woman, and Scot, in the post's 400-year history. She has published numerous collections of poetry for both adults and children, including *Mean Time* (1993), which won the Forward Prize; *The World's Wife* (1999); *Rapture* (2005), winner of the T. S. Eliot Prize; and *The Bees* (2011), winner of the 2011 Costa Poetry Award. She is also an acclaimed playwright.

Douglas Dunn (1942–) is best known for his poems depicting working-class life in Britain. He worked in libraries before graduating from the University of Hull, where he was an assistant librarian under Philip Larkin. His first collection, *Terry Street* (1969), was praised for its portrayal of working-class Hull. His acclaimed *Elegies* (1985), which won the Whitbread Book Award, was a poignant account of his first wife's death.

Stephen Dunn (1939–) was born in New York City and has had careers as a basketball player, literary editor, advertising copy-writer and teacher of creative writing. He has published fifteen collections of poetry and won the Pulitzer Prize for his 2001 collection *Different Hours*. His honours and awards include a fellowship from the National Endowment for the Arts, the James Wright Prize and an Academy Award for Literature.

Paul Durcan (1944–) was born in Dublin and is renowned as an outspoken chronicler and critic of life in Ireland. His work is satirical, surreal and politically engaged. In 1974 he won the

Patrick Kavanagh Award and published his first collection, *O Westport in the Light of Asia Minor*, in 1975. His 1990 collection *Daddy, Daddy* won the Whitbread Poetry Award.

Richard Eberhart (1904–2005) was an American poet and playwright who published numerous books of poetry. He won the Pulitzer Prize for *Selected Poems, 1930–1965* and the 1977 National Book Award for *Collected Poems, 1930–1976*. His poetry combines stylistic modernism with a Romantic sensibility and nature and death are recurring themes.

T. S. Eliot (1888–1965) was an Anglo-American poet, publisher, playwright and critic, who came to define the modernist literary movement. *The Waste Land* (1922) is widely regarded as the most influential work of poetry of the twentieth century. The publication of *Four Quartets* solidified his reputation as the greatest living English poet, and he was awarded both the Order of Merit and the Nobel Prize for Literature in 1948.

Martina Evans (1961–) grew up in County Cork and trained in Dublin as a radiographer before moving to London in 1988. She is the author of eleven books of poetry and prose. Her collection *Burnfort, Las Vegas* (2014) was shortlisted for the Irish Times Poetry Now Award, and her latest book, *Now We Can Talk Openly About Men* was selected as one of the best books of 2018 in the *TLS*, *Irish Times* and *Observer*.

Vicki Feaver (1943–) was born in Nottingham and her poetry often reflects her experience of growing up 'in a house of quarrelling women'. Her second collection, *The Handless Maiden* (1994), included both the Arvon International Poetry Competition finalist

'Lily Pond', and 'Judith', winner of the Forward Prize for Best Single Poem. Her 2006 collection *The Book of Blood* was shortlisted for the Costa Poetry Award.

Matthew Francis (1956–) is the author of five poetry collections published by Faber & Faber, most recently *The Mabinogi* (2017). He has twice been shortlisted for the Forward Prize and was chosen as one of the Next Generation poets in 2004. He has also published a collection of short stories and two novels, and edited W. S. Graham's *New Collected Poems*.

Robert Frost (1874–1963) was a highly celebrated American poet whose work is known for its depictions of rural New England life and for its skilful use of colloquial speech. He won four Pulitzer Prizes and recited a poem at the inauguration of President J. F. Kennedy, who had often quoted Frost at the end of his campaign speeches: 'But I have promises to keep / And miles to go before I sleep'.

W. S. Graham (1918–1986) was largely overlooked during his lifetime, but his reputation has been steadily growing in recent years. He was born in Scotland to a working-class family, and spent much of his adult life in Cornwall, associated with the artists' colony in St Ives. His playful and highly original poetry often reflects on the difficulties of language and communication.

Thom Gunn (1929–2004) was born in Gravesend, Kent, and his early poetry was associated with the English poets of The Movement, including Philip Larkin and Donald Davie. He emigrated to the US in 1954 to teach at Stanford University and lived in San Francisco from 1960 until his death. His later poetry combines English formality with American idiom and explores the themes of homosexuality and drug use.

Jen Hadfield (1978–) became the youngest person to win the T. S. Eliot Prize, for her second collection, *Nigh-No-Place*, in 2008. Her work is inspired by her experiences of living and working in Shetland. She won the Edwin Morgan Poetry Competition in 2012 and her third collection, *Byssus*, was published by Picador in 2014. She is also a visual artist and bookmaker.

Thomas Hardy (1840–1928) is almost unique in being equally revered as a poet and novelist. As a young man he worked as an architectural apprentice in London, but it was the rural south-west that provided him with most of the material for his writing. His lyric poetry is characterised by a highly original style which fuses modernist ideas with conventional poetic traditions.

Olav H. Hauge (1908–1994) was one of the most significant Norwegian poets of the twentieth century, and his work has been translated into more than twenty languages. He lived his whole life in Ulvik, Hordaland, trained as a horticulturalist and worked as a gardener in his own apple orchard. He wrote modernist and concrete poetry and was an important translator of poetry from English, German and French.

Seamus Heaney (1939–2013) was born in County Derry, Northern Ireland, and his poetry is notable for its evocations of Irish history, mythology and rural life. He was the author of over twenty volumes of poetry and criticism and won the Nobel Prize for Literature in 1995 'for works of lyrical beauty and ethical depth, which exalt everyday miracles and the living past.' He taught at Harvard University and was Oxford Professor of Poetry from 1989 to 1994.

Anthony Hecht (1923–2004) was born in New York City and his work is noted for its skilful mastery of traditional poetic forms. He fought in the Second World War and his writing confronts many of the horrors of twentieth-century history, with the Holocaust a recurrent theme. He was awarded the Pulitzer Prize in 1968 for his second collection, *The Hard Hours*.

George Herbert (1593–1633) is known for his religious poetry and is regarded as one of the most important British devotional lyricists. His writing is associated with the Metaphysical poets and is characterised by its linguistic precision, playful rhythms and inventive use of imagery and conceits. His collection *The Temple* was published shortly after his death in 1633, with an introduction by Nicholas Ferrar.

Robert Herrick (1591–1674) was born in London, the seventh child of a wealthy goldsmith who committed suicide in 1592. Herrick was ordained as a priest in 1623 and mixed in literary circles, with Ben Jonson among his acquaintances. He published only one collection, *Hesperides*, in 1648, which contained about 1,400 poems, many of them short and epigrammatic.

Selima Hill (1945–) was raised on farms in England and Wales, surrounded by creative parents and grandparents, who were all painters. Her poetry combines psychological intensity with whimsical humour and is often brilliantly surreal in its imagery. Fiona Sampson called Hill 'arguably the most distinctive truth-teller to emerge in British poetry since Sylvia Plath'. Her work has been shortlisted for the Forward Prizes, the T. S. Eliot Prize and the Whitbread Poetry Award.

Gerard Manley Hopkins (1844–1889) is regarded as one of the great poets of the Victorian era, though it was not until after his death that his achievements were acknowledged. After joining a Jesuit novitiate in 1868, he burned his youthful poetry and vowed to 'write no more'. His first collection was published posthumously, in 1918, and his work is now recognised as among the most original and influential in modern poetry.

Ted Hughes (1930–1998) was born into a working-class family in West Yorkshire. His poetry is characterised by its unsentimental, anthropological approach to the cruel brutality of animal life. He married the American poet Sylvia Plath in 1956 and was deeply affected by her suicide in 1963. His collections include *Wodwo* (1967), *Crow* (1970), *Wolfwatching* (1989) and *Birthday Letters* (1998). He was poet laureate from 1984 until his death.

T. E. Hulme (1883–1917) was born in Endon, England, and killed in action during the First World War. The headstone on his grave memorialises him as 'One of the War Poets'. Though few of his poems were published during his lifetime, he was one of the founders of the imagist movement and an important figure in twentieth-century modernist poetry.

Rolf Jacobsen (1907–1994) was born in Oslo, Norway, and is one of Scandinavia's most acclaimed poets, regarded by many as the first Norwegian modernist writer. His debut collection, *Jord og jern* (1933), written in free verse, introduced his interest in modern, industrial subjects and his exploration of the complex relationship between nature and technology. His poetry has been translated into more than twenty languages.

Kathleen Jamie (1962–) was born in Renfrewshire and studied philosophy at the University of Edinburgh. She received an Eric Gregory award in 1981, publishing her first collection, *Black Spiders*, in 1982. Her poetry is rooted in Scottish landscapes and culture. *The Tree House* (2004) won the Forward Prize and *The Overhaul* (2012) was shortlisted for the T. S. Eliot Prize and won the Costa Award for Poetry.

Laura Kasischke (1961–) is a Professor of English Language and Literature at the University of Michigan. Her numerous collections of poetry include *Wild Brides* (1992), *Fire and Flower* (1998), *Gardening in the Dark* (2004), *Space, in Chains* (2011), which won the National Book Critics Circle Award, and *Where Now* (2017). She is also a novelist and has received fellowships from the Guggenheim Foundation and the National Endowment for the Arts.

John Keats (1795–1821) was an English lyric poet who, in his short life, wrote a remarkable number of poems which helped define the Romantic tradition. The sensual imagery that characterises his poetry is most memorably displayed in his famous series of odes. During his brief career he took on the challenges of a wide range of poetic forms, and his poetry is among the most anthologised in English literature. He died of tuberculosis at the age of twenty-five.

Ted Kooser (1939–) is known for his honest, accessible verse which captures a quotidian way of life through its conversational style. Deeply influenced by the people and landscape of the American Midwest, his poetry records a way of life that is disappearing. He won the Pulitzer Prize in 2005 for his collection *Delights and Shadows*, and in 2004 became the first poet from the Great Plains to be named US poet laureate.

James Lasdun (1958–) was born in London and has lived in the US since 1986, and his work often reflects on the disparities between the cultures and landscapes of these two countries. He has published four collections of poetry, including *Landscape with Chainsaw* (2001), which was shortlisted for the T. S. Eliot and Forward Prizes. He is also a novelist and screenwriter and has taught at Princeton, New York and Columbia universities.

Denise Levertov (1923–1997) grew up in Ilford, Essex. She moved to the US in 1948 and became associated with the poets of the Black Mountain school. Her poetry is characterised by the spare immediacy of its simple, concrete language, and avoidance of metaphor and allusion. She was politically active during the 1960s and '70s, when her poetry became more socially conscious.

Norman MacCaig (1910–1996) was born in Edinburgh and made his living as a primary school teacher. He was a conscientious objector during the Second World War and a pacifist throughout his life. His early work is associated with the surrealism of the New Apocalypse movement, while his later work is defined by its spare and disciplined style. His awards included an OBE and the Queen's Medal for Poetry.

Louis MacNeice (1907–1963) was born in Belfast and studied at the University of Oxford where he was a contemporary of

W. H. Auden and Stephen Spender, with whom his work is often associated. He was less overtly political than Auden or Spender, and his writing is characterised by its familiar, often humorous tone, and a pride in his Irish heritage. He found an audience for his work through British radio and wrote many successful radio verse plays.

Derek Mahon (1941–) was born in Belfast to Ulster Protestant working-class parents. He studied at Trinity College Dublin and at the Sorbonne in Paris. His work explores contemporary subjects through classical poetic forms, and reflects the influence of W. H. Auden and Louis MacNeice. He has influenced a younger generation of British, Irish and Scandinavian poets.

John Masefield (1878–1967) was born in Ledbury in Herefordshire, and spent his early adult life at sea, which provided the inspiration for some of his best-known poems from his first collection, *Salt-Water Ballads* (1902). He is also known for his long narrative poems, including *The Everlasting Mercy* (1911), which shocked the literary establishment with its bawdy colloquialism. He was Poet Laureate from 1930 until his death.

Glyn Maxwell (1962–) read English at the University of Oxford and won a scholarship to Boston University where he studied poetry and drama with Derek Walcott. He is known for his innovative work across genres, as a poet, playwright, librettist and novelist. Four of his collections have been shortlisted for the T. S. Eliot Prize and two for the Whitbread Poetry Prize. Recent collections include *The Sugar Mile* (2005) and *Pluto* (2013).

Charlotte Mew (1869–1928) spent her whole life, except for brief holidays, living in and around the Bloomsbury district of

London, and was regarded as one of the best poets of her age by fellow writers. Thomas Hardy described her as 'Far and away the best living woman poet – who will be remembered when others are forgotten.' She wrote a number of dramatic monologues, for which she adopted the voices of various personae, both male and female. Several of her poems are spoken in a West Country dialect.

Marianne Moore (1887–1972) was born in Kirkwood, Missouri, and was one of America's foremost modernist poets. She was a disciplined craftsman, and her poetry is formally and linguistically precise, characterised by its acute observations and descriptions. She was the editor of the influential literary magazine *Dial* from 1925 to 1929. Her *Collected Poems* (1951) won both the Pulitzer Prize and the National Book Award.

Sinead Morrissey (1972–) grew up in Northern Ireland and was Belfast's inaugural poet laureate. She has published six collections of poetry, including *Parallax*, which won the 2013 T. S. Eliot Prize, and *On Balance*, which won the 2017 Forward Prize for Best Collection. Her work is alert to its historical context, while remaining highly inquisitive and formally inventive.

Daljit Nagra (1966–) was born in London to Indian immigrant parents and much of his work reflects on the experiences of British-born Indians, often playing with Punjabi-inflected English. His poem 'Look We Have Coming to Dover!' won the Forward Prize for Best Individual Poem in 2004 and his collection of the same name won the Forward Prize for Best First Collection in 2007.

Bernard O'Donoghue (1945–) was born in County Cork, Ireland, and moved to Manchester when he was sixteen. He studied

Medieval English at the University of Oxford, where he later taught medieval and Irish literature until his retirement. His most recent poetry collections are *Farmers Cross* (2011) and *The Seasons of Cullen Church* (2016), both of which were shortlisted for the T. S. Eliot Prize.

Frank O'Hara (1926–1966) was one of the most energetic and distinguished of the New York School of poets, whose work drew inspiration from abstract expressionism, jazz, surrealism and action painting. 'A poet among painters', he worked as a curator at the Museum of Modern Art. He devised a poetic style that attempted to linguistically mirror the effects the artists around him had created on canvas.

Mary Oliver (1935–) was born in Maple Heights, Ohio, and her work draws heavily on her childhood, and the landscape of her adopted home in New England. Her poetry is firmly rooted in the natural world and a Romantic approach to nature, exploring the intersection between the human and natural worlds. She was awarded the Pulitzer Prize for her collection *American Primitive* (1983).

Alice Oswald (1966–) studied classics at the University of Oxford and worked as a gardener for a number of years. Her poetry is deeply engaged with the rhythms of the land and the natural environment, and her language shows an affinity with the characters and oral traditions of classical literature. She has been the recipient of every major poetry prize in the UK and her latest collection, *Falling Awake* (2016), won the Griffin Poetry Prize.

Rebecca Perry (1986–) graduated from Manchester's Centre for New Writing in 2008. Her first full collection, *Beauty/Beauty*, was published by Bloodaxe in 2015 and was shortlisted for the Fenton Aldeburgh Prize for Best First Collection and the T. S. Eliot Prize. She edits the online journal *Poems in Which* and was Writer Fellow at the University of Manchester in 2016.

Marge Piercy (1936–) was born in Detroit, Michigan, and grew up in a working-class Jewish family that had been seriously affected by the Depression. A prolific poet and novelist, she has published nearly twenty books of poetry. A committed Marxist, feminist and environmentalist, her work explores the ideology and aesthetic of these causes. Her collection *The Moon is Always Female* (1980) is considered a seminal feminist text.

Katherine Pierpoint (1961–) spent her early career in publishing and television before becoming a full-time writer, editor and translator. Her first collection, *Truffle Beds* (1995), won a Somerset Maugham Award and was shortlisted for the T. S. Eliot Prize. In 1996 she was named *Sunday Times* Young Writer of the Year. Her translation, with Tom Boll, of Mexican poet Coral Bracho's *Poems* was published in 2008.

Sylvia Plath (1932–1963) was born in Boston, Massachusetts, and studied at the University of Cambridge where she met her future husband Ted Hughes. Her work played a significant role in developing the genre of confessional poetry and she is best known for her collections *The Colossus and Other Poems* (1960) and *Ariel* (1965). She suffered from episodes of severe depression through-out her life and committed suicide aged 30. In 1982 she became the first poet to be posthumously awarded the Pulitzer Prize.

Christopher Reid (1949–) was born in Hong Kong and educated in England. His numerous poetry books include *A Scattering* (winner of the 2009 Costa Book of the Year Award) and *The Song of Lunch*, a book-length poem that was dramatised for BBC television. From 1991 to 1999 he was Poetry Editor at Faber & Faber. He is often cited as co-founder, with Craig Raine, of the 'Martian School' of poetry, which uses exotic and humorous metaphors to defamiliarise the everyday.

Denise Riley (1948–) was born in Carlisle and is known for her ability to combine philosophy, feminist theory, lyric and literary history in books of poetry and prose. Her influence is increasingly widely felt among younger generations of poets, and her 2016 collection *Say Something Back* was shortlisted for the Forward Prize, the Costa Poetry Award and the T. S. Eliot Prize.

Maurice Riordan (1953–) was born in Lisgoold, County Cork, and is a teacher, poet, translator and editor. His collections include *A Word from the Loki* (1995), which was shortlisted for the T. S. Eliot Prize, and *Floods* (2000) which was shortlisted for the Whitbread Poetry Award. He was Editor of *Poetry London* from 2005 to 2009 and Editor of *The Poetry Review* from 2013 to 2017.

Dante Gabriel Rossetti (1828–1882) was an English painter and poet and a founding member of the Pre-Raphaelite Brotherhood, a movement which revolted against contemporary trends in British painting to promote the art of serious subjects treated with precise realism. Poetry and image are closely linked in Rossetti's work, which influenced the European Symbolists and was an important precursor to the Aesthetic movement.

Kay Ryan (1945–) was US poet laureate from 2008 to 2010. Her collections of poetry include *Flamingo Watching* (2006), *The Niagara River* (2005) and *Say Uncle* (2000). *The Best of It: New and Selected Poems* (2010) won the Pulitzer Prize for Poetry. She is often referred to as a poetry 'outsider' and her style has been compared to that of Emily Dickinson and Marianne Moore.

Anne Sexton (1928–1974) was known for her intimate, confessional verse, drawing on her experiences of mental illness and details of her private life. She was first encouraged to write poetry by her therapist. Her writing met with instant success, and she remained an extremely popular writer until her suicide at the age of 46. In 1967 she received the Pulitzer Prize for her collection *Live or Die* (1966).

William Shakespeare (1564–1616) is best known for his plays but was equally revered as a poet during his lifetime. London's theatres were often closed due to the plague between 1592 and 1594, and it was during that time that Shakespeare dedicated himself to writing his longer narrative poems. His sonnets are perhaps his most famous works of poetry and *The Sonnets of Shakespeare* – consisting of 154 sonnets written in the form now known as the Shakespearean sonnet – was published in 1609.

Charles Simic (1938–) was born in Belgrade in former Yugoslavia and emigrated to the US in 1954. He won the Pulitzer Prize in 1990 for his book of prose poems *The World Doesn't End*. He was appointed the fifteenth Poet Laureate Consultant in Poetry in 2007 and was the recipient of the 2011 Frost Medal for 'lifetime achievement in poetry'.

Jean Sprackland (1962–) is a Senior Lecturer in Creative Writing at Manchester Metropolitan University, and a trustee of the Poetry Archive. Her first collection, *Tattoos for Mother's Day* (1997), was shortlisted for the Forward Prize for Best First Collection, her second collection, *Hard Water* (2003), for the T. S. Eliot Prize, and in 2007 she won the Costa Poetry Award for her third collection, *Tilt*.

Mark Strand (1934–2014) was a Canadian-born American poet, essayist and translator. His poetry is characterised by its deceptively spare, simple language and surreal, often elegiac imagery. He was named poet laureate of the United States in 1990 and won the Pulitzer Prize for his collection *Blizzard of One* in 1998. He taught English and comparative literature at Columbia University from 2005 until his death in 2014.

Edward Thomas (1878–1917) wrote all of his poetry in just three years, before he was killed in action in the First World War. He was a successful essayist and literary critic before he began writing poetry, encouraged by his close friend, the American poet Robert Frost. His verse concerns itself with the influence of war on the natural order, and is cherished today for an intensity of vision that sets him apart from many of his contemporaries. Most of his poems were published posthumously.

Derek Walcott (1930–2017) was born in the former British colony of Saint Lucia, an island in the West Indies. He trained as a painter but soon focused his attention on writing. His work moves between Caribbean patois and English and his breakthrough collection, *In a Green Night: Poems 1948–1960* (1962), celebrates the Caribbean and its history, and the scars of colonialism. He was awarded the Nobel Prize for Literature in 1992.

Ethelwyn Wetherald (1857–1940), daughter of two English Quakers, was born in Ontario, Canada, and spent most of her childhood on the family's fruit and dairy farm in Fenwick. She began her writing career as a journalist and proofreader for a number of periodicals, to which she also contributed short stories and poems. Having published her first poem in a magazine at the age of seventeen, she was to wait over thirty years before her first book of poetry, *The House of the Trees and Other Poems*, appeared in 1895. Later in life she returned to the family farm, where she found fresh inspiration for her final three books of poems.

Dorothy Wordsworth (1771–1855) was a poet and prose writer, and sister of the Romantic poet William Wordsworth. Although she did not publish her work during her lifetime, many of her journals, travelogues and poems have been posthumously collected and published. She was an avid naturalist, and much of her writing explores the natural world.

William Wordsworth (1770–1850) was born in the Lake District and much of his poetry is concerned with the relationship between nature and the human mind. The publication of *Lyrical Ballads* (1798), written with Samuel Taylor Coleridge, helped launch the English Romantic movement, establishing a new style, vocabulary and subject for poetry. His great autobiographical poem, *The Prelude*, was published shortly after his death.

James Wright (1927–1980) was born in Martin's Ferry, Ohio, and his work draws on the poverty and suffering he witnessed as a child, engaging with profound and often sorrowful human experiences. *The Branch Will Not Break* (1963), which marked a turning point in his career, had a significant influence on many

American poets writing in the 1960s and '70s. He won the Pulitzer Prize in 1972 for his *Collected Poems*.

W. B. Yeats (1865–1939) was the son of Anglo-Irish landowning parents, and was involved with the Celtic Revival, a movement against the influences of English rule in Ireland. His cultural roots remained strong throughout his life, and he often drew on Irish mythology and folklore in his work. He also had an abiding interest in spiritualism and the occult. He received the Nobel Prize for Literature in 1923.

Jane Yeh was born in New Jersey, educated at Harvard and, since 2002, has lived in London. Her first collection *Marabou* (2005) was nominated for the Whitbread, Forward, and Aldeburgh poetry prizes. She has since published two further collections: *The Ninjas* (2012) and *Discipline* (2019). Carol Rumens has written in *The Guardian* of 'the guiltless, almost jubilant acceptance' of the anthropomorphism of a number of Yeh's animal poems. She has won numerous awards for her poetry and was named a Next Generation poet by the Poetry Book Society in 2014.

Andrew Young (1885–1971) was born in Elgin, Scotland, and spent most of his adult life in Sussex, working as a poet and clergyman. He was influenced by the Metaphysical poets, and much of his poetry was based on his observations of nature and wildlife. Notable collections include *Winter Harvest* (1933) and *Speak to the Earth* (1939). He also published a number of prose books about poetry, botany and landscape.

Kevin Young (1970–) was born in Lincoln, Nebraska, and studied with Seamus Heaney and Lucie Brock-Broido at Harvard. His collections include *Brown* (2018), *Blue Laws: Selected and Uncollected Poems 1995–2015* (2016) and *Book of Hours* (2014), winner of the 2015 Lenore Marshall Poetry Prize. He is Poetry Editor of the *New Yorker* and Director of New York Public Library's Schomburg Centre for Research in Black Culture.

Acknowledgements

With warm thanks to Anthony Cheetham for setting me on this journey, to Helen Francis, Ellen Parnavelas and the rest of the team at Head of Zeus, and to my agent, Georgina Capel, for her ready support and wise words. Thank you, too, to my husband, Andrew Stevenson, for his love, patience, humour and insight, and for his close reading of this book in an earlier form.

Index of Poets

Index of Titles and First Lines

Extended Copyright

Adcock, Fleur: 'For a Five-Year-Old' from *Poems 1960–2000* (Bloodaxe, 2000). Reprinted by permission of Bloodaxe Books © Fleur Adcock, 2000.

Armitage, Simon: 'Zoom!' from *Zoom!* (Bloodaxe, 1989). Reprinted by permission of Bloodaxe Books © Simon Armitage, 1989.

Benson, Fiona: 'Poem for James' from *Bright Travellers* (Cape Poetry, 2014). Reprinted by permission of the author c/o Rogers, Coleridge & White Ltd. © Fiona Benson, 2014.

Berry, Emily: 'Canopy' from *Stranger, Baby* (Faber, 2017). Reprinted by permission of Faber & Faber Ltd. © Emily Berry, 2017.

Bly, Robert: 'Taking the Hands' from *Silence in the Snowy Fields* (first published 1962, reprinted by Wesleyan University Press, 2011). Reprinted by permission of Wesleyan University Press © Robert Bly, 1962.

Browning, Robert: 'Meeting at Night' and 'Now'. These works are in the public domain.

Bryce, Colette: 'A Spider' from *Self-Portrait in the Dark* (Picador, 2008). Reprinted by permission of Picador © Colette Bryce, 2008.

Cavendish, Margaret: 'Of Many Worlds in this World'. This work is in the public domain.

Clare, John: 'Sudden Shower'. This work is in the public domain.

Constantine, David: 'As our bloods separate' from *Collected Poems*

(Bloodaxe, 2006). Reprinted by permission of Bloodaxe Books © David Constantine, 2006.

Creeley, Robert: 'I Know a Man' from *Selected Poems 1945–1990* (Marion Boyars, 1991). Reprinted by permission of Marion Boyars Publishers © Robert Creeley 1991.

Crichton-Smith, Iain: 'Tinily a Star Goes Down' from *Collected Poems* (Carcanet, 1995). Reprinted by permission of Carcanet © Iain Crichton-Smith, 1995.

Daryush, Elizabeth: 'Still-Life' from *Modern Women Poets*, ed. Deryn Rees-Jones (Bloodaxe, 2005). Reprinted by permission of Bloodaxe Books © Elizabeth Dayrush, 2005.

Day Lewis, C.: 'Walking Away'. This work is in the public domain.

Dickinson, Emily: 'The Brain – is wider than the Sky –' and 'I'm nobody! Who are you?'. These works are in the public domain.

Donne, John: 'The Sunne Rising'. This work is in the public domain.

Douglas, Keith: 'Behaviour of Fish in an Egyptian Tea Garden' from *Simplify Me When I'm Dead: Poems Selected by Ted Hughes* (Faber, 2010). Reprinted by permission of Farrar, Straus and Giroux © 1964 by The Estate of Keith Douglas. Introduction and selection © 1964 by The Estate of Ted Hughes.

Dove, Rita: 'Daystar' from *Collected Poems: 1974–2004* (Norton, 2016) © Rita Dove, 2016.

Duffy, Carol Ann: 'Words, Wide Night' from *New Selected Poems, 1984–2004* (Picador, 2004). Reprinted by permission of the author c/o Rogers, Coleridge & White Ltd. © Carol Anne Duffy 2004.

Dunn, Douglas: 'On Roofs of Terry Street' from *Selected Poems* (Faber, 2003). Reprinted by permission of Faber & Faber Ltd. © Douglas Dunn, 2003.

Dunn, Stephen: 'Summer Nocturne' from *What Goes On* (Norton,

2013). Reprinted by permission of W. W. Norton & Company, Inc. © Stephen Dunn, 2006.

Eberhart, Richard: 'At Night' from *Collected Poems 1930–1986* (Oxford University Press; Revised edition, 1988) © Richard Eberhart, 1988.

Eliot, T. S.: 'Prelude I' from *The Waste Land and Other Poems* (Faber, 1972). Reprinted by permission of Faber & Faber Ltd. © T. S. Eliot, 1972.

Evans, Martina: 'The Room' from *The Windows of Graceland* (Carcanet, 2016). Reprinted by permission of Carcanet Press © Martina Evans 2016.

Feaver, Vicki: 'Ironing' from *The Handless Maiden* (Jonathan Cape, 1994). Reprinted by permission of The Random House Group Limited. © Vicki Feaver 1994.

Francis, Matthew: 'Ant' first published in *Poetry* magazine 2014. Reprinted by permission of the author © Matthew Francis, 2014.

Frost, Robert: 'Stopping by Woods on a Snowy Evening' and 'Birches' from *Selected Poems* (Penguin, 1969). Reprinted by permission of The Random House Group Limited © Robert Frost, 1969.

Graham, W. S.: 'Lines on Roger Hilton's Watch' from *Selected Poems* (Faber, 1996) © W. S. Graham, 1996.

Gunn, Thom: 'The Hug' from *Collected Poems* (Faber, 1993). Reprinted by permission of Faber & Faber Ltd. © Thom Gunn, 1993.

Hadfield, Jen: 'Daed-traa' and 'Cabbage' from *Nigh-No-Place* (Bloodaxe, 2008). Reprinted by permission of Bloodaxe Books © Jen Hadfield 2008. 'Lichen' from *Byssus* (Picador, 2014).

Hardy, Thomas: 'A Thunderstorm In Town' from *The Complete Poems*, ed. James Gibson (Macmillan, 1976). This work is in the public domain.

Hauge, Olav H.: (tr. Robin Fulton) 'Leaf-Huts and Snow-Houses' from *Leaf-Huts and Snow-Houses: Selected Poems* (Anvil Press Poetry, 2003). Reprinted by permission of Carcanet © Olav H. Hague, 2003.

Heaney, Seamus: 'Sunlight (from Mossbawn: Two Poems in Dedication)' from *New Selected Poems 1966–1987* (Faber, 1990). Reprinted by permission of Faber & Faber Ltd. © Seamus Heaney, 1990.

Hecht, Anthony: 'A Hill' from *The Hard Hours* (New York: Atheneum, 1967) © Anthony Hecht, 1967.

Herbert, George: 'Love' from *The Oxford Book of Twentieth-Century Verse* (OUP, 1973). This work is in the public domain.

Herrick, Robert: 'The Bracelet: To Julia' from *The Oxford Book of Twentieth Century Verse* (OUP, 1973). This work is in the public domain.

Hill, Selima: 'Being a Wife' from Gloria: Selected Poems (Bloodaxe, 2008). Reprinted by permission of Bloodaxe Books © Selima Hill 2008.

Hopkins, Gerard Manley: 'Repeat that, repeat', 'Heaven-Haven' and 'The Windhover' from *Gerard Manley Hopkins: Poems and Prose* (Penguin Classics, 1985) and *The Poems of Gerard Manley Hopkins*, ed. Gardner & Mackenzie (OUP, 1967). These works are in the public domain.

Hughes, Ted: 'A Cranefly in September', 'Full Moon and Little Frieda' from *Selected Poems: 1957–1981* (Faber, 1982). Reprinted by permission of Faber & Faber Ltd. © Ted Hughes, 1982.

Hulme, T. E.: 'Autumn'. This work is in the public domain.

Jacobsen, Rolf: (tr. Roger Greenwald): 'Rubber' from *North in the World* (University of Chicago Press, 2002). Reprinted by permission of University of Chicago Press © Rolf Jacobsen, 2002.

Jamie, Kathleen: 'Blossom' from *The Bonniest Companie* (London:

Picador, 2015). Reprinted by permission of Picador © Kathleen Jaime, 2015.

Kasischke, Laura: 'Ivan' from *Where Now: New and Selected Poems* (Copper Canyon Press , 2004). Reprinted with the permission of The Permissions Company, Inc. on behalf of Copper Canyon Press, www.coppercanyonpress.org. © Laura Kasischke, 2004.

Keats, John: 'After dark vapours have oppressed our plains' from *The Complete Poems*, ed. John Barnard (Penguin, 1973) and 'To Sleep'. These works are in the public domain.

Kooser, Ted: 'A Rainy Morning' from *Delights & Shadows* (Copper Canyon Press, 2004). Reprinted with the permission of The Permissions Company, Inc. on behalf of Copper Canyon Press, www.coppercanyonpress.org. © Ted Kooser, 2004.

Levertov, Denise: 'Laying the Dust' from *Denise Levertov: New Selected Poems*, ed. Paul A. Lacey (Bloodaxe, 2003). Reprinted by permission of Bloodaxe Books © Denise Levertov 2003.

MacCaig, Norman: 'Summer Farm' from *The Oxford Book of Twentieth-Century Verse* (OUP, 1973). This work is in the public domain.

MacNeice, Louis: 'Snow' from *Selected Poems of Louis MacNeice* (Faber & Faber, 1964) © Louis MacNeice, 1964.

Mahon, Derek: 'Everything Is Going To Be All Right' from *Selected Poems* (The Gallery Press, 1993). Reprinted by permission of the author and The Gallery Press © Derek Mahon, 1993.

Masefield, John: 'Sea-Fever' from *The Oxford Book of Twentieth-Century Verse* (OUP, 1973). Reprinted by permission of The Society of Authors as the Literary Representation of John Masefield © John Masefield, 1973.

Maxwell, Glyn: 'Stargazing' from *One Thousand Nights and Counting* (Picador, 2011) © Glyn Maxwell, 2011.

Mew, Charlotte: 'Wright' from *Charlotte Mew: Complete Poems* (ed.